A Journey of Grace

100 DAYS OF DEVOTION & PRAYER

FIND HOPE AND STRENGTH ROOTED IN GOD'S PROMISES

THIS BOOK BELONGS TO :

_____

_____

_____

_____

WOMEN WHO PRAY

DEDICATION

To the incredible women who seek God with steadfast hearts,

This book is dedicated to you—each one of you who walks in faith, seeking His presence with sincerity and grace. Your dedication to pursuing God's will and embracing His promises is a beacon of hope and encouragement. May this devotional be a source of strength and inspiration as you continue your journey, finding joy and peace in His unwavering love and faithfulness.

With deep respect and gratitude.

—Women Who Pray—

INTRODUCTION

Welcome to this journey of spiritual growth and reflection. This devotional is designed to be a companion for your daily walk with God, offering moments of inspiration, encouragement, and connection with His Word. As you embark on this journey, our hope is that each devotion will draw you closer to the heart of God and enrich your faith.

PURPOSE OF THE DEVOTIONAL: The primary purpose of this devotional is to guide you through a series of reflections based on Scripture that will nurture your relationship with God. Each entry is crafted to help you:
Deepen Your Understanding: By exploring specific Bible verses, you'll gain insight into God's character, His promises, and His purposes for your life.

STRENGTHEN YOUR FAITH: Through daily encouragement, you'll find strength and courage to face the challenges of life, grounded in the truth of God's Word.

FOSTER SPIRITUAL GROWTH: The reflections and applications are designed to help you grow in your relationship with God, encouraging you to live out your faith in practical ways.

HOW TO USE
THIS DEVOTIONAL

DAILY READING: Set aside a specific time each day to read the devotion. Whether it's in the morning to start your day or in the evening to reflect on your day, consistency is key.

PRAYER AND REFLECTION: After reading the devotional, take a moment to pray and reflect. Ask God to speak to you through the Scripture and to apply His truths to your life.

CONTEMPLATION: Consider how you can incorporate the insights from each devotion into your daily life. Look for ways to live out the lessons learned and to grow in your walk with Christ.

JOURNALING: Use the space provided to jot down your thoughts, prayers, and any insights you gain in the 20 pages at the end of the book. Journaling can be a powerful tool for spiritual reflection and growth.

ENCOURAGEMENT

As you journey through this devotional, remember that God is with you every step of the way. His Word is a lamp to your feet and a light to your path (Psalm 119:105). Trust in His guidance, lean on His promises, and open your heart to the transformative power of His love.

May this devotional be a source of hope, inspiration, and spiritual renewal. We pray that as you engage with these reflections, you will experience a deeper sense of God's presence and an increased passion for His kingdom.

Welcome to this adventure of faith. May it lead you to a richer and more vibrant relationship with our Lord and Savior.

100-DAY CHRISTIAN
Devotional for Women

DAY 01
Strength in Christ
Philippians 4:13 (NKJV)
"I can do all things through Christ who strengthens me."

Devotional

Today's verse is a powerful reminder of the boundless strength and support we receive through Christ. It's easy to feel overwhelmed by life's challenges, whether personal struggles, professional obstacles, or relational difficulties. But this verse assures us that no matter how daunting our circumstances may seem, we have access to a strength that transcends our limitations.

Paul wrote this verse while facing hardships and uncertainties. Despite being imprisoned and enduring various trials, he found his confidence and resilience in Christ. His faith was not in his abilities or resources but in the sustaining power of Jesus. This perspective invites us to rely not on our strength, but on the strength that Christ provides.

Prayer

Lord,

Thank You for the incredible promise that I can do all things through Christ who strengthens me. I admit that I often rely on my strength, which is limited and frail. Today, I surrender my challenges to You and ask for Your strength to fill me. Help me to approach each task with confidence, knowing that You are my source of power and resilience. May Your strength be evident in my life, and may it inspire others to trust in You as well.
In Jesus' name, Amen.

CONTEMPLATION

Spend a few quiet moments in meditation, envisioning yourself empowered by Christ's strength. Let His presence fill you with peace and confidence as you face the day ahead.

DAY 02
Renewed Strength

Isaiah 40:31 (NIV)

"But those who hope in the Lord will renew their strength. They will soar on wings like eagles; they will run and not grow weary, they will walk and not be faint."

Devotional

In a world that often leaves us feeling exhausted and drained, this verse from Isaiah offers a powerful promise of renewal and strength. The imagery of soaring on wings like eagles is particularly striking—eagles are known for their majestic flight and ability to rise above storms. This metaphor highlights the spiritual renewal and elevation that comes from placing our hope and trust in the Lord.

Isaiah 40:31 was written to a people in exile, feeling weary and hopeless. Yet, it speaks of a profound truth that resonates across ages: our strength and endurance come not from our efforts, but from our reliance on God. When we place our hope in Him, He revitalizes us, empowering us to rise above life's challenges and continue moving forward with perseverance.

Prayer

Heavenly Father,

I come to You feeling weary and in need of renewal. Your promise in Isaiah 40:31 reminds me that my strength comes from You and that through hope in You, I can be uplifted and empowered. Please renew my strength today, Lord. Help me to rise above my challenges, to run without growing weary, and to walk without fainting. Fill me with Your peace and power, and guide me in Your ways. Thank You for being my source of strength and hope.

In Jesus' name, Amen.

CONTEMPLATION

Take a few moments to sit quietly and meditate on the image of soaring like an eagle. Feel the weight of your burdens lift as you envision yourself being carried by God's strength. Let this moment of contemplation bring you peace and renewed hope.

DAY 03
Trusting God's Plans

Jeremiah 29:11 (NIV)

"For I know the plans I have for you," declares the Lord, "plans to prosper you and not to harm you, plans to give you hope and a future."

Devotional

In times of uncertainty or when facing difficult decisions, it's easy to become anxious about the future. This verse from Jeremiah serves as a profound reminder of God's sovereign and loving plan for each of us. The Israelites, to whom this promise was originally given, were in exile, feeling lost and hopeless. Yet, God assured them that despite their current circumstances, He had a purposeful plan that would lead to a hopeful future.

Jeremiah 29:11 speaks to the heart of God's intentions for us. His plans are not just for survival but for prosperity and hope. This doesn't mean life will always be easy or straightforward, but it assures us that God's ultimate purpose for our lives is good. When we place our trust in Him, we align ourselves with His divine plan, which surpasses our limited understanding.

Prayer

Heavenly Father,

Thank You for the reassuring promise of Jeremiah 29:11. In moments of uncertainty and doubt, I am comforted by the knowledge that You have a plan for my life that is full of hope and promise. Please help me to trust in Your plans, even when I cannot see the way forward. Fill me with Your peace and guide me according to Your will. Strengthen my faith and help me to live each day with hope and confidence in Your goodness. In Jesus' name, Amen.

CONTEMPLATION

Spend a few quiet moments meditating on the fact that God has a specific, loving plan for your life. Visualize yourself trusting in His plan and feeling a sense of peace and hope. Let the reassurance of His promise sink in, knowing that He is guiding you towards a future filled with His goodness and purpose. Allow this contemplation to instill a renewed sense of hope and trust as you go about your day.

DAY 04
Comfort in Our Brokenness

Psalm 34:18 (NIV)

"The Lord is close to the brokenhearted and saves those who are crushed in spirit."

Devotional

Life is filled with moments of brokenness and heartache, and it's during these times that we might feel the most isolated or overwhelmed. Psalm 34:18 offers a profound comfort by reminding us that God draws near to those who are hurting. This verse assures us that God is not distant or indifferent to our pain. Instead, He is close, offering His presence and saving grace to those who are struggling.

The imagery of God being close to the brokenhearted is especially poignant. It suggests an intimate and compassionate response from God. He is not merely observing from afar but is actively involved in healing and restoring us when we are at our lowest. Whether our brokenness comes from loss, disappointment, or personal failure, God's promise is to be near and to save us from our distress.

Prayer

Heavenly Father,
I am grateful for Your promise in Psalm 34:18 that You are close to the brokenhearted and save those who are crushed in spirit. In my moments of pain and heartache, help me to feel Your comforting presence. Please heal my brokenness and restore my spirit. Surround me with Your peace and strength as I navigate through these challenging times. Thank You for being a compassionate and caring God who never leaves my side.
In Jesus' name, Amen.

CONTEMPLATION

Spend a few moments in silence, focusing on the comforting presence of God. Visualize Him drawing near to you and imagine His peace enveloping you. Let this time of contemplation reassure you of His closeness and care.

DAY 05
Trusting God's Goodness

Romans 8:28 (NIV)

"And we know that in all things God works for the good of those who love him, who have been called according to his purpose."

Devotional

Romans 8:28 is a powerful affirmation of God's promise to work everything in our lives for good. This verse reassures us that no matter the circumstances we face, God is actively involved in orchestrating everything with our ultimate good in mind. It's a profound reminder that even in the midst of trials, setbacks, or uncertainties, God's love and purpose are at work.

The key to understanding this promise lies in the phrase "those who love him." This indicates that the verse is directed towards those who have committed their lives to God and seek to follow His will. For those individuals, God is continually working behind the scenes, turning even challenging situations into opportunities for growth and blessing.

Prayer

Heavenly Father,

Thank You for the promise in Romans 8:28 that You work all things together for good for those who love You. In times of difficulty and uncertainty, help me to trust in Your goodness and Your plan for my life. Give me eyes to see the ways You are working behind the scenes and the faith to believe that You are always at work for my benefit. Strengthen me with Your peace and patience as I wait for Your perfect timing. Thank You for Your unwavering love and purpose.

In Jesus' name, Amen.

CONTEMPLATION

Spend a few moments in quiet reflection, considering the ways in which God might be working for your good in your current circumstances. Allow this contemplation to strengthen your trust in His plan and bring you comfort in His promises.

DAY 06
Finding Refuge in God

Psalm 46:1 (NIV)
"God is our refuge and strength, an ever-present help in trouble."

Devotional

Psalm 46:1 offers a profound promise of God's presence and support during times of difficulty. The verse describes God as both our refuge and strength, highlighting two critical aspects of His character that are especially comforting when we face challenges.

A refuge is a place of safety and shelter from danger or distress. In times of trouble, God is our safe haven, providing us with a sense of security and peace. Strength denotes His ability to support and uphold us, giving us the power to endure and overcome obstacles. The verse also assures us that God is "ever-present," meaning He is always with us, regardless of the circumstances.

When life feels overwhelming, this verse invites us to turn to God as our refuge and strength. It encourages us to seek His presence and rely on His power to sustain us. By doing so, we can experience His peace and find the resilience we need to face any challenge.

DAY 06
Finding Refuge in God

Psalm 46:1 (NIV)
"God is our refuge and strength, an ever-present help in trouble."

Devotional

Psalm 46:1 offers a profound promise of God's presence and support during times of difficulty. The verse describes God as both our refuge and strength, highlighting two critical aspects of His character that are especially comforting when we face challenges.

A refuge is a place of safety and shelter from danger or distress. In times of trouble, God is our safe haven, providing us with a sense of security and peace. Strength denotes His ability to support and uphold us, giving us the power to endure and overcome obstacles. The verse also assures us that God is "ever-present," meaning He is always with us, regardless of the circumstances.

When life feels overwhelming, this verse invites us to turn to God as our refuge and strength. It encourages us to seek His presence and rely on His power to sustain us. By doing so, we can experience His peace and find the resilience we need to face any challenge.

Prayer

Dear Lord,

I am grateful for the promise of Psalm 46:1 that You are our refuge and strength, an ever-present help in trouble. When I face challenges and difficulties, help me to turn to You for safety and support. Strengthen me with Your power and grant me the peace that comes from knowing You are always with me. May I find comfort in Your presence and confidence in Your ability to sustain me. Thank You for being my unwavering refuge and strength.

In Jesus' name, Amen.

CONTEMPLATION

Spend a few moments in quiet reflection, focusing on God as your refuge and strength. Visualize yourself taking refuge in Him, feeling His protective and sustaining presence. Let this contemplation bring you peace and reassurance as you face the day.

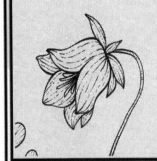

DAY 07
Finding Peace Through Prayer

Philippians 4:6-7 (NIV)

"Do not be anxious about anything, but in every situation, by prayer and petition, with thanksgiving, present your requests to God. And the peace of God, which transcends all understanding, will guard your hearts and your minds in Christ Jesus."

Devotional

In the midst of life's uncertainties and anxieties, Philippians 4:6-7 offers a comforting and practical approach to finding peace. The Apostle Paul encourages us to replace anxiety with prayer, presenting our concerns to God through prayer and petition. This invitation to communicate with God is not just about asking for help but also about expressing gratitude and trust in His goodness.

The promise here is profound: when we bring our requests to God with a thankful heart, His peace—beyond human comprehension—will guard our hearts and minds. This peace is not based on our circumstances but on our relationship with Christ. It acts as a protective barrier, keeping us calm and secure despite the chaos around us.

Prayer

Heavenly Father,
Thank You for the promise in Philippians 4:6-7 that You will guard my heart and mind with Your peace when I present my worries to You. I come to You with my anxieties and concerns, trusting in Your power and goodness. Help me to pray with a thankful heart, acknowledging Your past blessings and trusting in Your future provision. Fill me with Your peace that surpasses all understanding and protect my heart and mind in Christ Jesus.
In His name, Amen.

CONTEMPLATION

Spend a few moments in silence, focusing on the peace of God. Visualize His peace surrounding and protecting you, allowing it to calm your worries and bring a sense of tranquility. Let this moment of contemplation deepen your trust in His promise.

DAY 08
Strength in Weakness

2 Corinthians 12:9 (NIV)
"But he said to me, 'My grace is sufficient for you, for my power is made perfect in weakness.' Therefore I will boast all the more gladly about my weaknesses, so that Christ's power may rest on me."

Devotional

In 2 Corinthians 12:9, the Apostle Paul shares a profound lesson he learned about God's grace and power. Paul had asked God three times to remove a "thorn in his flesh," a persistent problem or weakness that troubled him. Instead of removing it, God responded with a powerful truth: "My grace is sufficient for you."

This verse highlights a significant spiritual principle: God's power is most evident when we acknowledge and embrace our weaknesses. Our struggles and limitations are opportunities for God's grace to shine through. When we are weak, we are more likely to rely on God, making room for His strength to be displayed in our lives.

Paul's response to this revelation was to boast about his weaknesses. This might seem counterintuitive, but it underscores the idea that our imperfections are platforms for showcasing God's grace. When we embrace our weaknesses and rely on God, His power is magnified.

Prayer

Lord,
Thank You for the promise of 2 Corinthians 12:9 that Your grace is sufficient for me and that Your power is made perfect in my weaknesses. I often struggle with feelings of inadequacy and limitation, but I am comforted by the truth that You are strong where I am weak. Help me to embrace my weaknesses and rely on Your strength. May Your power be evident in my life, and may I find peace and confidence in Your grace.
In Jesus' name, Amen.

CONTEMPLATION

Spend a few moments in quiet reflection, focusing on how God's grace can cover your weaknesses. Imagine His power being made perfect in the areas where you feel most inadequate. Let this contemplation bring you comfort and strength as you recognize His grace at work in your life.

DAY 09
Fear Not, For I Am With You

Isaiah 41:10 (NIV)

"So do not fear, for I am with you; do not be dismayed, for I am your God. I will strengthen you and help you; I will uphold you with my righteous right hand."

Devotional

Isaiah 41:10 is a comforting promise from God, offering reassurance and strength in times of fear and uncertainty. The verse starts with a clear command: "Do not fear." Fear often arises from the unknown or from feeling inadequate in the face of challenges. Yet, God's response to our fear is both a promise and an invitation to trust in His presence and power.

God assures us of His constant presence with the words "I am with you." This is not a distant or passive presence but an active one that strengthens, helps, and upholds us. The imagery of God's "righteous right hand" conveys both His authority and His support. It signifies that His guidance and protection are both just and powerful.

When we face trials or feel overwhelmed, this verse reminds us that we are not alone. God's strength is available to us, and He will support us through every difficulty. By trusting in His presence and promises, we can find courage and reassurance.

Prayer

Heavenly Father,

Thank You for the reassuring promise of Isaiah 41:10. I am comforted by Your promise that You are with me, that You will strengthen and help me, and that You will uphold me with Your righteous right hand. Help me to trust in Your presence and power when I feel afraid or dismayed. Fill me with courage and peace, knowing that I am never alone. May Your strength be evident in my life and may I be a source of encouragement to others.

In Jesus' name, Amen.

CONTEMPLATION

Spend a few moments in silence, focusing on the comforting presence of God. Visualize Him upholding you with His righteous right hand, providing strength and support. Let this time of contemplation fill you with peace and confidence as you face the day.

DAY 10
New Mercies Every Morning

Lamentations 3:22-23 (NIV)

"Because of the Lord's great love we are not consumed, for his compassions never fail. They are new every morning; great is your faithfulness."

Devotional

Lamentations 3:22-23 offers a profound reminder of God's unwavering love and faithfulness. The context of this verse is significant: it was written during a time of deep suffering and lament, yet it speaks of hope and renewal. Despite the challenges and pain experienced, the writer reflects on the unchanging nature of God's compassion.

The phrase "because of the Lord's great love we are not consumed" highlights that God's love is the reason we can face each day, regardless of our circumstances. His compassion, which "never fails," is a constant source of strength and comfort. The assurance that His mercies are "new every morning" means that each day is an opportunity to experience His fresh grace and renewal.

This verse encourages us to start each day with the knowledge that God's love and compassion are renewed daily. No matter what happened yesterday or what challenges lie ahead, we can find hope and strength in the fact that God's faithfulness is constant and His mercies are always available.

Prayer

Heavenly Father,
I am grateful for the promise of Lamentations 3:22-23 that Your mercies are new every morning and that Your faithfulness is great. Thank You for Your constant love and compassion, which sustain me through each day. Help me to start this day with a heart full of gratitude and trust in Your renewal and grace. As I face challenges, may I remember that Your mercy is always available and that Your faithfulness never wavers.
In Jesus' name, Amen.

CONTEMPLATION

Spend a few quiet moments reflecting on the freshness of God's mercies. Visualize the new beginning each day brings and let this contemplation fill you with peace and encouragement as you move forward with renewed hope.

DAY 11

The Lord Is Our Shepherd

Psalm 23:1 (NIV)
"The Lord is my shepherd, I lack nothing."

Devotional

Psalm 23:1 opens with one of the most comforting and well-known statements in Scripture: "The Lord is my shepherd." This simple yet profound declaration carries deep significance. To call the Lord our Shepherd is to acknowledge Him as the one who guides, provides for, and cares for us. In ancient times, a shepherd's role was crucial—guiding the flock to green pastures, providing water, and protecting them from danger. The image of God as our Shepherd underscores His intimate involvement in our lives.

The verse goes on to say, "I lack nothing." This doesn't mean that every desire will be fulfilled, but rather that with God as our Shepherd, our essential needs are met. His guidance ensures we are led to what is truly good for us, and His provision covers all that we truly need. This promise invites us to trust in His care and find contentment in His provision.

Prayer

Dear Lord,

Thank You for being my Shepherd and for the promise of Psalm 23:1 that I lack nothing when You are guiding and providing for me. Help me to trust in Your care and provision, knowing that You meet my essential needs and lead me to what is truly good. Teach me to find contentment in Your blessings and to rely on Your guidance. May I be a source of encouragement to others by sharing the assurance of Your provision.

In Jesus' name, Amen.

CONTEMPLATION

Take a few moments to meditate on the image of God as your Shepherd. Visualize yourself being led to green pastures and beside still waters. Let this contemplation bring you peace and reassurance, knowing that you are under the care of a loving and attentive Shepherd.

DAY 12
Overflowing with Hope

Romans 15:13 (NIV)
"May the God of hope fill you with all joy and peace as you trust in him, so that you may overflow with hope by the power of the Holy Spirit."

Devotional

Romans 15:13 is a beautiful benediction that offers a powerful message of hope, joy, and peace. The verse begins by referring to God as the "God of hope," emphasizing that all hope originates from Him. This hope is not just a fleeting or superficial feeling but a deep, abiding confidence rooted in God's promises and His character.

The verse promises that as we trust in God, He will fill us with "all joy and peace." This joy and peace are not dependent on external circumstances but are a result of our trust in God's faithfulness. As we place our trust in Him, His joy and peace become a natural outpouring in our lives.

The culmination of this promise is that we "overflow with hope by the power of the Holy Spirit." The image of overflowing suggests an abundance that cannot be contained. It indicates that the hope we receive from God is so plentiful that it spills over into every area of our lives, impacting others and transforming our outlook.

Prayer

Heavenly Father,

I am grateful for Your promise in Romans 15:13 that You are the God of hope and that You fill us with all joy and peace as we trust in You. Help me to place my full trust in You and to experience the abundant joy and peace that comes from Your presence. May Your hope overflow in my life, touching those around me and transforming my outlook. Fill me with the power of the Holy Spirit so that I may live in the fullness of Your hope.

In Jesus' name, Amen.

CONTEMPLATION

Spend a few moments in quiet reflection, focusing on the concept of overflowing hope. Imagine God's hope filling you to the point of overflowing, affecting every aspect of your life. Let this contemplation renew your spirit and strengthen your faith in His promises.

DAY 13
Strength for Every Challenge

Philippians 4:13 (NIV)
"I can do all this through him who gives me strength."

Devotional

Philippians 4:13 is a powerful reminder of the strength that comes from Christ. The Apostle Paul, who wrote this verse, had experienced a wide range of circumstances, from times of abundance to periods of need. Through it all, he learned that his strength did not come from his own abilities but from Christ.

The phrase "I can do all this" refers to the ability to face any situation, whether it's a challenge, a change, or a task, through the strength provided by Christ. This verse is not about being able to do anything we set our minds to, but about relying on Jesus for strength to handle whatever life brings our way.

Understanding that our strength comes from Christ shifts our focus from our own limitations to His infinite power. This verse encourages us to face difficulties with confidence, knowing that Christ empowers us to endure and overcome.

Prayer

Lord Jesus,
Thank You for the promise in Philippians 4:13 that I can do all things through You who gives me strength. When I face difficulties or feel overwhelmed, help me to remember that my strength comes from You and not from my own abilities. Empower me to handle each challenge with confidence and grace. May Your strength be evident in my life, and may I be a source of encouragement to others who need to rely on Your power.
In Jesus' name, Amen.

CONTEMPLATION

Spend a few moments in quiet reflection, focusing on the strength that Christ provides. Visualize His strength supporting you in your current challenges. Let this time of contemplation fill you with confidence and peace, knowing that with Christ, you have the power to overcome.

DAY 14
Casting Your Cares on Him

1 Peter 5:7 (NIV)
"Cast all your anxiety on Him because He cares for you."

Devotional

1 Peter 5:7 is a beautiful reminder of God's tender care and our call to release our anxieties into His hands. The verse opens with a clear instruction: "Cast all your anxiety on him." This call to action implies a deliberate choice to hand over our worries and stresses rather than trying to handle them on our own.

The reason we are encouraged to cast our anxieties on God is because "He cares for you." This assurance is not just a passive statement but a profound declaration of God's active concern for our well-being. It implies that our burdens are not too heavy for Him and that He is deeply invested in our lives.

When we take our anxieties to God, we are acknowledging our dependence on Him and trusting in His ability to handle our concerns. This act of surrender can bring relief and peace, knowing that we are not alone in our struggles.

Prayer

Dear Heavenly Father,
Thank You for the promise of 1 Peter 5:7 that I can cast all my anxieties on You because You care for me. I bring my worries and concerns before You now, trusting in Your love and ability to handle them. Help me to release my anxieties into Your hands and to find peace in Your care. Strengthen my faith as I surrender my concerns to You, and remind me of Your constant presence in my life .
In Jesus' name, Amen.

CONTEMPLATION

Spend a few moments in quiet reflection, visualizing yourself handing over your anxieties to God. Imagine His comforting presence enveloping you and carrying your burdens. Let this time of contemplation bring you a sense of relief and assurance, knowing that your cares are in His capable hands.

DAY 15
Finding Stillness in God

Psalm 46:10 (NIV)
"Be still, and know that I am God; I will be exalted among the nations, I will be exalted in the earth."

Devotional

Psalm 46:10 offers a profound invitation to find peace and assurance in the presence of God. In a world that often feels chaotic and demanding, this verse encourages us to pause and acknowledge the sovereignty and power of God.

The command to "be still" is more than just a call for physical quietness. It's an invitation to quiet our hearts and minds, to let go of our anxieties and busyness, and to focus on the fact that God is in control. In stillness, we can reconnect with God's presence and trust in His authority.

The promise that God will be "exalted among the nations" and "exalted in the earth" reminds us that, despite the turbulence we may face, God's ultimate plan is one of victory and sovereignty. When we take time to be still and recognize God's supremacy, we find reassurance that He is working in all things, even when we cannot see it.

Prayer

Lord,
I thank You for the promise in Psalm 46:10 to "be still" and know
that You are God. Help me to find moments of stillness amidst
the busyness of life and to trust in Your sovereignty and power.
When I feel overwhelmed, remind me that You are exalted and
in control of all things. Grant me Your peace and assurance as I
place my trust in You. May I reflect Your calm and trust in my
interactions with others.
In Jesus' name, Amen.

CONTEMPLATION

Spend a few moments in quiet contemplation, focusing
on the stillness and peace that comes from knowing
God is in control. Allow this sense of calm to envelop
you, reinforcing your trust in His sovereign authority
and care.

DAY 16
Unchanging Faithfulness

Malachi 3:6 (NIV)
"I the Lord do not change. So you, the descendants of Jacob, are not destroyed."

Devotional

Malachi 3:6 is a powerful reminder of the unchanging nature of God. In this verse, God declares, "I the Lord do not change." This statement is foundational to our understanding of His faithfulness and reliability. Unlike the shifting circumstances of life or the changing attitudes of people, God remains constant and unalterable.

The promise that follows this declaration is equally profound: "So you, the descendants of Jacob, are not destroyed." Despite the Israelites' unfaithfulness and their frequent departures from God's ways, His unchanging nature ensured that His covenant promises remained intact. His commitment to them was unwavering, and this same commitment extends to us today.

In times of uncertainty or personal struggle, this truth can be a source of immense comfort. Knowing that God's character does not fluctuate with our circumstances gives us a stable anchor for our faith. His love, mercy, and promises are as steadfast as He is.

Prayer

Heavenly Father,
I thank You for the assurance in Malachi 3:6 that You do not change. Your faithfulness and love remain constant, and Your promises are steadfast. Help me to trust in Your unchanging nature and find comfort in Your reliability. When I face uncertainties and challenges, remind me that You are my stable anchor and that I am secure in Your unchanging grace. May Your faithfulness give me peace and confidence as I navigate through life.
In Jesus' name, Amen.

CONTEMPLATION

Spend a few moments in quiet reflection, focusing on the constancy of God's nature. Imagine His unchanging love and promises surrounding you, providing a steady foundation. Allow this contemplation to bring you peace and reassurance, knowing that God's faithfulness remains steadfast regardless of life's fluctuations.

DAY 17
Embracing God's Compassion

Psalm 103:8 (NIV)
"The Lord is compassionate and gracious, slow to anger, abounding in love."

Devotional

Psalm 103:8 provides a beautiful description of God's character. It emphasizes four key attributes: compassion, grace, patience, and love. This verse paints a vivid picture of how God interacts with us, revealing His nature as one who is deeply empathetic and forgiving.

COMPASSIONATE AND GRACIOUS: God's compassion means He understands our suffering and responds with kindness. His grace is His unearned favor, extending forgiveness and blessings that we don't deserve but desperately need. Together, these qualities remind us that God is not distant or detached, but intimately involved in our lives with a heart full of mercy.

SLOW TO ANGER: God's patience is a testament to His understanding and forbearance. He does not react impulsively or harshly but gives us time to turn back to Him and grow. His patience ensures that we are given opportunities to change and learn, rather than being met with immediate judgment.

ABOUNDING IN LOVE: God's love is overflowing and abundant. It is not limited or conditional but is a constant, unwavering force in our lives. His love encompasses us, surrounds us, and provides a foundation of security and hope.

Prayer

Dear Lord,
Thank You for being compassionate and gracious, slow to anger, and abounding in love. I am grateful for Your kindness and patience with me, and for the abundant love You continually pour into my life. Help me to reflect Your character in my interactions with others, showing compassion and grace. As I face challenges today, remind me of Your unwavering love and let it be a source of strength and comfort. May I extend the same love and patience to those around me, living out the truth of Your attributes in all I do.
In Jesus' name, Amen.

CONTEMPLATION

Spend a few moments in quiet reflection, focusing on each of God's attributes mentioned in Psalm 103:8. Visualize His compassion, grace, patience, and love enveloping you. Let this time of contemplation renew your sense of His care and inspire you to embody these qualities in your own life.

DAY 18
The Eternal Plans of God

Psalm 33:11 (NIV)
"But the plans of the Lord stand firm forever, the purposes of his heart through all generations."

Devotional

Psalm 33:11 offers a profound reassurance about the nature of God's plans and purposes. In a world where change is constant and uncertainties abound, this verse reminds us that God's plans are unchanging and eternal. His purposes are not swayed by time or circumstance but remain steadfast through every generation.

The verse begins with "But the plans of the Lord stand firm forever." This is a powerful declaration of God's unshakeable intent and commitment. Unlike human plans, which can be altered or disrupted, God's plans are secure and unwavering. This firmness gives us a solid foundation to build our lives upon, knowing that His purposes are not only reliable but also enduring.

Furthermore, "the purposes of his heart through all generations" underscores that God's intentions are driven by His eternal love and wisdom. His purposes span beyond our individual lifetimes and encompass the entirety of human history. This long-term perspective offers us comfort and assurance that God's work is both purposeful and perpetual.

Prayer

Heavenly Father,
Thank You for the promise in Psalm 33:11 that Your plans stand firm forever and that the purposes of Your heart endure through all generations. I am grateful for the certainty and security Your unchanging plans provide. Help me to trust in Your eternal purposes, even when I face uncertainties or challenges. May Your steadfastness be a source of comfort and hope for me today. Guide me to align my plans with Yours and to find peace in knowing that Your purposes are always good. In Jesus' name, Amen.

CONTEMPLATION

Spend a few moments in quiet reflection, focusing on the eternal nature of God's plans. Visualize His unchanging purposes enveloping your life, providing stability and assurance. Let this time of contemplation deepen your trust in His eternal wisdom and strengthen your hope in His unchanging nature.

DAY 19
The Depth of God's Love

John 3:16 (NIV)

"For God so loved the world that he gave his one and only Son, that whoever believes in him shall not perish but have eternal life."

Devotional

John 3:16 is one of the most well-known and beloved verses in the Bible, capturing the essence of God's profound love for humanity. This verse is a cornerstone of Christian faith, illustrating the incredible depth and breadth of God's love and the promise of eternal life through Jesus Christ.

The verse begins with, "For God so loved the world." This statement encompasses the entire human race, emphasizing that God's love is not limited by boundaries or conditions. It is a love that reaches out to every individual, regardless of their past or present circumstances.

The verse goes on to say that God "gave his one and only Son." This sacrifice is the ultimate expression of love, showing that God was willing to give up His most precious possession for our benefit. Jesus' sacrificial death on the cross and subsequent resurrection provide the means for us to receive forgiveness and eternal life.

Finally, the promise that "whoever believes in him shall not perish but have eternal life" offers a clear invitation. Belief in Jesus is not just an intellectual acknowledgment but a heartfelt trust in His redemptive work. This belief ensures that we are granted eternal life—a life in perfect relationship with God, free from the consequences of sin and death.

Prayer

Heavenly Father,
I am in awe of the depth of Your love as revealed in John 3:16. Thank You for giving Your one and only Son so that I might have eternal life. Help me to fully grasp the significance of this incredible sacrifice and to live in the light of Your love. Strengthen my faith and enable me to reflect Your love in my interactions with others. May I share this message of hope and salvation with those around me, so they too may experience the gift of eternal life through Jesus Christ.
In Jesus' name, Amen.

CONTEMPLATION

Spend a few moments in quiet reflection, focusing on the magnitude of God's love expressed through Jesus. Allow this contemplation to deepen your sense of gratitude and inspire you to live in a way that honors the sacrifice made for you. Let this time bring you peace and confidence in the eternal life you have through belief in Christ.

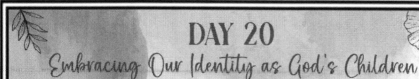

DAY 20
Embracing Our Identity as God's Children

Galatians 4:6 (NIV)
"Because you are his children, God sent the Spirit of his Son into our hearts, the Spirit who calls out, 'Abba, Father.'"

Devotional

Galatians 4:6 is a profound reminder of our intimate relationship with God through Jesus Christ. This verse highlights the transformative reality of being adopted into God's family and the role of the Holy Spirit in affirming our identity as His beloved children.

"Because you are his children" speaks to the core of our new identity in Christ. Through faith in Jesus, we are not just forgiven but also embraced as sons and daughters of God. This familial relationship is marked by love, acceptance, and a deep connection with our Heavenly Father.

The verse continues with, "God sent the Spirit of his Son into our hearts." This is a powerful truth about the Holy Spirit's role in our lives. The Spirit's presence is a constant reminder of our belonging and the reality of our relationship with God. The Spirit's cry, "Abba, Father," reflects a personal and affectionate address to God, much like a child calling out to a loving parent.

Understanding this verse encourages us to live with the confidence and security of being God's children. It reassures us of our place in His family and the intimacy of our relationship with Him.

Prayer

Heavenly Father,
I am deeply grateful for the truth of Galatians 4:6 that You have adopted me as Your child and sent Your Spirit into my heart. I thank You for the intimate relationship I have with You and for the assurance of Your constant love and presence. Help me to fully embrace my identity as Your beloved child and to live with the confidence and peace that comes from knowing I am deeply loved by You. May Your Spirit guide and comfort me each day, and may I reflect Your love in my interactions with others.
In Jesus' name, Amen.

CONTEMPLATION

Spend a few moments in quiet contemplation, focusing on the sense of security and love that comes from being a child of God. Picture yourself drawing near to your Heavenly Father with the confidence and trust of a beloved child. Let this time of reflection deepen your connection with God and fill you with His peace and assurance.

DAY 21
Embracing Our Inheritance in Christ

Galatians 3:29 (NIV)
"If you belong to Christ, then you are Abraham's seed, and heirs according to the promise."

Devotional

Galatians 3:29 reveals a profound truth about our identity and inheritance through Jesus Christ. This verse emphasizes that, through our faith in Christ, we are not only connected to the promises made to Abraham but are also rightful heirs to those promises.

The phrase "If you belong to Christ" highlights the crucial condition for this inheritance. Belonging to Christ means that we are united with Him, sharing in His identity and blessings. This union transforms us from mere believers into full participants in God's grand plan.

The verse continues, "then you are Abraham's seed." This statement connects us to the promises God made to Abraham, the father of faith. Abraham was promised that through his offspring, all nations would be blessed (Genesis 22:18). By belonging to Christ, we are included in this promise. We become part of a spiritual lineage that receives the blessings of God's covenant.

"...and heirs according to the promise." This concluding phrase assures us that, as heirs, we inherit not only the blessings of God's kingdom but also His promises of love, guidance, and eternal life. This inheritance is a testament to God's faithfulness and His desire for us to live in the fullness of His blessings.

Understanding Galatians 3:29 invites us to embrace our identity as heirs of God's promises. It encourages us to live confidently, knowing that we have been included in God's grand plan and that His promises are assured to us through our relationship with Christ.

Prayer

Heavenly Father,
I am grateful for the truth in Galatians 3:29 that through faith in Christ, I am an heir to Your promises. Thank You for including me in the blessings You promised to Abraham and for making me part of Your spiritual family. Help me to fully embrace my identity as Your child and to live with the confidence that comes from knowing I am an heir according to Your promise. May this truth guide my actions and interactions, and may I share this assurance with others.
In Jesus' name, Amen.

CONTEMPLATION

As you go through your day, remember that you are a part of God's grand promise. Live with the assurance that His blessings and love are yours, and seek ways to be a blessing to others as a testament to His grace.

DAY 22
A Transformed Heart

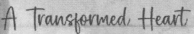

Ezekiel 36:26-27 (NIV)
"I will give you a new heart and put a new spirit in you; I will remove from you your heart of stone and give you a heart of flesh. And I will put my Spirit in you and move you to follow my decrees and be careful to keep my laws."

Devotional

Ezekiel 36:26-27 offers a powerful promise of transformation and renewal from God. In these verses, God speaks through the prophet Ezekiel, revealing His commitment to change and heal our innermost being.

The promise begins with, "I will give you a new heart and put a new spirit in you." This signifies a profound internal change. A "new heart" represents a heart that is responsive and tender towards God, replacing the "heart of stone" that is resistant and unfeeling. The "new spirit" symbolizes the fresh perspective and vitality that God imparts to us, enabling us to live in alignment with His will.

God also promises to "remove from you your heart of stone." This transformation is essential for overcoming the hardened attitudes and resistance that can keep us distant from Him. By giving us a "heart of flesh," God makes our hearts more sensitive and open to His guidance and love.

Additionally, "I will put my Spirit in you" assures us of the gift of the Holy Spirit, who empowers us to live according to God's ways. The Spirit helps us to "follow my decrees" and be "careful to keep my laws." This means that through the Spirit's work in our lives, we are not only transformed internally but also enabled to live out the principles of God's kingdom.

Understanding these verses encourages us to embrace the new life that God offers. It reminds us that transformation is possible and that God's Spirit is actively at work in our hearts, guiding us to live according to His will.

Prayer

Heavenly Father,
I am grateful for the promise in Ezekiel 36:26-27 that You will give me a new heart and a new spirit. Thank You for removing my heart of stone and replacing it with a heart of flesh that is tender and responsive to Your love. Fill me with Your Spirit and guide me to follow Your decrees and live according to Your will. Help me to embrace this transformation and to reflect Your love and grace in all that I do.
In Jesus' name, Amen.

CONTEMPLATION

Spend a few moments in quiet reflection, focusing on the transformation God is working in your heart. Visualize yourself receiving a new heart and spirit from Him, and let this image deepen your sense of renewal and hope.

DAY 23
Finding Purpose in Every Situation

Philippians 1:13 (NIV)
"As a result, it has become clear throughout the whole palace guard and to everyone else that I am in chains for Christ."

Devotional

Philippians 1:13 captures a profound lesson in finding purpose and perspective in challenging circumstances. The Apostle Paul, writing from imprisonment, reveals how his chains have become a platform for proclaiming Christ. His imprisonment, rather than being a setback, has turned into a unique opportunity to spread the Gospel.

Paul's statement, "it has become clear throughout the whole palace guard," shows that his situation, while difficult, has not hindered his mission. Instead, it has amplified his witness. His unwavering faith and dedication to Christ have made his purpose evident even in the midst of suffering. The "palace guard" and "everyone else" have seen that Paul's chains are not merely a result of misfortune but are part of a larger divine plan.

This verse invites us to view our own difficulties through a lens of purpose. Whether we face challenges in our personal lives, careers, or relationships, we can find meaning in these trials by seeing them as opportunities to reflect God's light and share His love. Just as Paul's imprisonment advanced the Gospel, our struggles can become a testament to our faith and a way to influence those around us.

Prayer

Heavenly Father,
I thank You for the example of Paul and for the reminder in Philippians 1:13 that even in difficult circumstances, You have a purpose for us. Help me to view my current challenges through the lens of Your plan and to trust that You can use my situation to advance Your Kingdom. Give me the courage to remain faithful and to look for ways to reflect Your love and grace. May my trials be an opportunity to witness to others and to glorify You.
In Jesus' name, Amen.

CONTEMPLATION

Spend a few moments in quiet reflection, focusing on how your current circumstances might be used for God's purposes. Consider the ways you can remain steadfast in your faith and make a positive impact despite the challenges you face.

DAY 24
Finding Rest in God's Green Pastures

Psalm 23:2 (NIV)
"He makes me lie down in green pastures, he leads me beside quiet waters."

Devotional

Psalm 23:2 offers a serene and comforting image of God's care and provision. The verse paints a picture of peaceful rest and renewal, which is central to understanding our relationship with the Lord as our Shepherd.

The phrase "He makes me lie down in green pastures" evokes a sense of tranquility and abundance. Green pastures symbolize a place of nourishment and rest, where one can relax and be rejuvenated. In a world that often feels chaotic and demanding, this imagery reminds us that God invites us to pause and experience His provision and peace.

Similarly, "He leads me beside quiet waters" portrays a scene of calm and refreshment. Quiet waters are not only a source of physical nourishment but also a symbol of spiritual renewal. Just as still waters provide a moment of calm and reflection for a thirsty soul, so does God offer us spiritual refreshment and peace in His presence.

This verse encourages us to trust in God's ability to provide for our needs and to lead us to places of rest and renewal. It reminds us that in the midst of life's pressures and uncertainties, God offers us moments of peace and refreshment.

Prayer

Heavenly Father,
Thank You for the beautiful promise in Psalm 23:2 that You make me lie down in green pastures and lead me beside quiet waters. I am grateful for Your provision and the peace You offer in the midst of life's busyness. Help me to find rest in You and to trust in Your ability to renew and refresh my soul. Guide me to moments of calm and stillness where I can experience Your presence and peace. May I also share this comfort with others who need it.
In Jesus' name, Amen.

CONTEMPLATION

Spend a few moments in quiet reflection, focusing on the image of green pastures and quiet waters. Let this imagery deepen your sense of peace and assurance, and allow yourself to be refreshed by God's presence.

DAY 25
The Spirit Without Limit

John 3:34 (NIV)
"For the one whom God has sent speaks the words of God, for God gives the Spirit without limit."

Devotional

John 3:34 reveals a profound truth about the nature of Jesus and the generosity of God's Spirit. This verse highlights that Jesus, being sent by God, speaks with divine authority and insight, sharing God's words and truths with us. But the verse goes further, emphasizing that "God gives the Spirit without limit."

This concept of a Spirit without limit is deeply encouraging. It means that the Holy Spirit is not constrained or limited by human boundaries. Unlike human resources that can be depleted or restricted, the Spirit of God is abundant and freely available to us. This boundless gift signifies that God's presence, guidance, and empowerment are limitless.

In a world where we often experience limitations—whether in resources, time, or strength—this verse reminds us that God's Spirit operates beyond those constraints. He is always present, ready to guide, comfort, and empower us in every situation. The Spirit's presence is not rationed or restricted; it flows generously, providing us with the wisdom, strength, and peace we need.

Understanding this verse invites us to embrace the fullness of the Spirit's work in our lives. It encourages us to rely on the Spirit's unlimited resources and to seek His guidance and strength without hesitation or fear of running out.

Prayer

Heavenly Father,
Thank You for the promise in John 3:34 that You give the Spirit without limit. I am grateful for the boundless presence and power of Your Holy Spirit in my life. Help me to seek Your guidance and strength with confidence, knowing that Your Spirit is always available and abundant. Fill me with Your Spirit and use me to reflect Your love and wisdom to those around me. In Jesus' name, Amen.

CONTEMPLATION

Spend a few moments in quiet reflection, focusing on the limitless nature of the Holy Spirit. Allow this understanding to deepen your trust in God's provision and empower you to live with boldness and faith.

DAY 26
God's Steady Support

Psalm 37:24 (NIV)
"Though he may stumble, he will not fall, for the Lord upholds him with His hand."

Devotional

Psalm 37:24 provides a profound assurance of God's steadfast support and faithfulness. This verse is a comforting reminder that while we may face difficulties and stumble in our walk, we are never beyond God's reach or support.

The verse begins with, "Though he may stumble," acknowledging that even the most faithful among us can encounter moments of weakness and failure. Life's challenges can sometimes cause us to falter, and our path may not always be smooth. However, this verse assures us that such stumbles do not define our end.

The powerful promise follows: "he will not fall, for the Lord upholds him with His hand." Despite our stumbles, God's hand is steady and reliable. His support is unwavering, and He is always present to catch us when we fall. God's hand represents His protective and sustaining power. It is a reminder that we are held secure by His grace and strength, no matter the difficulties we face.

Understanding this verse encourages us to trust in God's continued support through our trials. It reminds us that God is our foundation, and even when we are weak, His strength upholds us. This assurance helps us face life's uncertainties with confidence, knowing that we are never alone and that God is with us every step of the way.

Prayer

Heavenly Father,

I am grateful for the promise in Psalm 37:24 that even though I may stumble, I will not fall because You uphold me with Your hand. Thank You for Your constant support and for being my foundation in times of trouble. Help me to trust in Your strength and to rely on Your guidance through every difficulty. May I feel Your steady presence and share this assurance with others who need encouragement.

In Jesus' name, Amen.

CONTEMPLATION

Spend a few moments in quiet reflection, focusing on God's promise to uphold you. Visualize His steady hand supporting and guiding you through your challenges. Let this vision deepen your trust in His unwavering support.

DAY 27
Equipped for Every Good Work

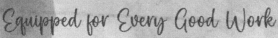

Hebrews 13:20-21 (NIV)

"Now may the God of peace, who through the blood of the eternal covenant brought back from the dead our Lord Jesus, that great Shepherd of the sheep, equip you with everything good for doing his will, and may he work in us what is pleasing to him, through Jesus Christ, to whom be glory for ever and ever. Amen."

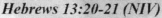

Devotional

Hebrews 13:20-21 offers a profound blessing and encouragement as we navigate our Christian journey. This passage highlights God's role as the source of peace and the One who equips us for every good work.

The verse begins by addressing "the God of peace," acknowledging that our peace comes from Him. This peace is grounded in the profound truth that "through the blood of the eternal covenant" Jesus, our Lord, was resurrected. This eternal covenant signifies a lasting and unbreakable relationship between God and us, secured through Christ's sacrifice and resurrection.

"Equip you with everything good for doing his will" is a powerful promise. It means that God doesn't just call us to do His will; He also provides us with the necessary tools, resources, and strength to fulfill it. Whatever task or challenge lies before us, God has already equipped us with everything we need to accomplish it.

Moreover, the verse speaks to God working in us to produce what is "pleasing to him." This means that God is actively involved in our lives, shaping and guiding us to align with His will and purpose. Our efforts are not in vain; He is working in and through us to bring about His good purposes.

Finally, the passage concludes with a doxology, giving "glory for ever and ever" to Jesus Christ. This reminder of eternal praise and worship helps us keep our focus on the ultimate goal: bringing glory to God through our lives.

Prayer

Heavenly Father,
I am grateful for the promise in Hebrews 13:20-21 that You are the God of peace who equips me for every good work. Thank You for the eternal covenant secured by the blood of Jesus and for providing me with everything I need to do Your will. Help me to trust in Your equipping, to allow You to work in my life, and to live in a way that brings glory to Jesus Christ. May my actions and attitudes reflect Your grace and purpose.
In Jesus' name, Amen.

CONTEMPLATION

Spend a few moments in quiet reflection, focusing on the ways God has equipped you and is working in your life. Consider how you can use this understanding to serve others and honor Him.

DAY 28
Embracing God's Loving Discipline

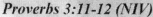

Proverbs 3:11-12 (NIV)

"My son, do not despise the Lord's discipline, and do not resent his rebuke, because the Lord disciplines those he loves, as a father the son he delights in."

Devotional

Proverbs 3:11-12 provides a deeply encouraging perspective on God's discipline. These verses remind us that God's correction is an expression of His love and care, much like a loving father guiding his child.

The instruction "do not despise the Lord's discipline" acknowledges that discipline, though challenging, is a vital part of our growth. It's natural to resist correction or feel uncomfortable when faced with it, but this passage encourages us to view discipline through the lens of love rather than punishment.

The reason given for embracing discipline is profound: "because the Lord disciplines those he loves." God's discipline is not arbitrary or harsh; it stems from His deep affection for us. Just as a father disciplines his child to guide and protect them, so God's correction is intended to steer us toward righteousness and away from harm. It's an act of love designed to help us grow in our faith and character.

The verse also highlights the joy and delight God takes in His children: "as a father the son he delights in." This imagery helps us understand that God's discipline is not about condemnation but about nurturing and refining us. His correction is a sign of His commitment to our well-being and spiritual growth.

Understanding this verse can transform our perspective on difficulties and challenges we face. Rather than viewing them as punitive, we can see them as opportunities for growth and deepening our relationship with God.

Prayer

Heavenly Father,
I thank You for the promise in Proverbs 3:11-12 that Your discipline is an expression of Your deep love for me. Help me to embrace Your correction with a heart open to growth and transformation. I trust that You are guiding me with Your loving hand and delighting in my development as Your child. Grant me the wisdom to see Your discipline as a path to greater faith and character.
In Jesus' name, Amen.

CONTEMPLATION

Spend a few moments in quiet reflection, considering how God's discipline has shaped your life. Allow yourself to experience gratitude for His loving guidance and commitment to your growth.

DAY 29
Embracing God's Blessing

Numbers 6:24-26 (NIV)
"The Lord bless you and keep you; the Lord make his face shine on you and be gracious to you; the Lord turn his face toward you and give you peace."

Devotional

Numbers 6:24-26 offers a beautiful blessing that captures the essence of God's care and favor towards His people. These verses, often referred to as the Aaronic Blessing, provide a rich assurance of God's protection, grace, and peace.

The blessing begins with, "The Lord bless you and keep you." This is a prayer for divine favor and protection. To be blessed by the Lord is to receive His goodness and grace in our lives, while to be kept by Him is to be safeguarded and watched over. It signifies that God is not only aware of our needs but actively involved in ensuring our well-being.

Next, the verse says, "The Lord make his face shine on you and be gracious to you." The imagery of God's face shining upon us signifies His pleasure and approval. It's an invitation to experience His kindness and favor. God's grace is unmerited and generous, and His shining face symbolizes His continual presence and support.

Finally, the blessing concludes with, "The Lord turn his face toward you and give you peace." The idea of God turning His face toward us implies intimacy and attentiveness. It means that God is fully present and engaged with us, offering His peace—a deep and abiding sense of tranquility that surpasses all understanding.

This verse reassures us that God's blessings are not just fleeting but are deeply rooted in His continual presence and care. No matter where we are or what we face, God's blessings encompass us, His grace sustains us, and His peace surrounds us.

Prayer

Heavenly Father,

I am grateful for the beautiful blessing in Numbers 6:24. Thank You for Your promise to bless me, keep me, and make Your face shine upon me. I receive Your grace and seek Your peace in my life. Help me to feel Your presence and experience Your favor in every situation. May Your peace, which surpasses all understanding, guard my heart and mind.

In Jesus' name, Amen.

CONTEMPLATION

Spend a few moments in quiet reflection, focusing on the aspects of God's blessing described in Numbers 6:24. Allow His grace and peace to fill you as you rest in His presence.

DAY 30
Finding God in the Search

Jeremiah 29:13 (NIV)
"You will seek me and find me when you seek me with all your heart."

Devotional

Jeremiah 29:13 is a profound promise from God that invites us into a deeper relationship with Him. This verse encapsulates the heart of God's desire for us to seek Him earnestly and wholeheartedly.

The verse begins with "You will seek me," which indicates an active pursuit. Seeking God is not a passive activity but a deliberate and intentional journey. It suggests that finding God requires effort and a genuine desire to know Him more intimately.

The promise that follows, "and find me," assures us of a divine response to our pursuit. God is not distant or hidden from us; He is available and eager to be discovered. This promise encourages us that our efforts to seek God will not be in vain. He is present and ready to reveal Himself to us.

The condition set forth, "when you seek me with all your heart," highlights the importance of sincerity and total commitment. God desires our wholehearted devotion. This means seeking Him not just in times of need but with a persistent and passionate heart. It involves aligning our entire being—our thoughts, emotions, and actions—toward finding and connecting with Him.

This verse encourages us to evaluate how we seek God in our daily lives. It invites us to pursue Him with a sincere heart and assures us that our pursuit will lead us to a deeper understanding and relationship with Him.

Prayer

Heavenly Father,
Thank You for the promise in Jeremiah 29:13 that I will find You when I seek You with all my heart. Help me to pursue You earnestly and wholeheartedly in every aspect of my life. Remove any distractions or half-hearted attempts and replace them with a sincere and passionate search for You. May Your presence be more evident in my life as I seek You daily.
In Jesus' name, Amen.

CONTEMPLATION

Spend a few moments in quiet reflection, focusing on your pursuit of God. Allow the promise of Jeremiah 29:13 to inspire you to seek Him with a deeper and more dedicated heart.

DAY 31

Embracing God's Goodness in the Midst of Trials

Psalm 97:10 (NIV)

"Let those who love the Lord hate evil, for he guards the lives of his faithful ones and delivers them from the hand of the wicked."

Devotional

Psalm 97:10 is a powerful reminder of God's protective nature and His call for us to align our lives with His goodness. This verse encapsulates a profound promise and a call to action for those who love the Lord.

The verse begins with, "Let those who love the Lord hate evil." This command reflects the idea that our love for God should influence our stance on moral and ethical issues. Loving God means rejecting what is contrary to His nature and His commands. It's a call for us to actively pursue righteousness and to distance ourselves from sin.

The promise that follows is a comforting assurance: "for he guards the lives of his faithful ones and delivers them from the hand of the wicked." Here, God's protective role is emphasized. He is portrayed as a vigilant guardian who watches over His faithful ones. This means that God is actively involved in safeguarding us from harm and delivering us from evil. His protection is not passive; it is a deliberate and active intervention in our lives.

Understanding this verse invites us to trust in God's ability to protect and deliver us, even in difficult situations. It encourages us to maintain our love for God and our commitment to His ways, knowing that He is our defender and rescuer.

Prayer

Heavenly Father,
I am grateful for the promise in Psalm 97:10 that You guard the lives of Your faithful ones and deliver them from the hand of the wicked. Help me to love You deeply and to hate what is evil. Strengthen my trust in Your protection and deliverance. Guide me to live righteously and to rely on Your vigilant care. May Your presence be a constant reassurance in times of trial.
In Jesus' name, Amen.

CONTEMPLATION

Spend a few moments in quiet reflection, focusing on God's protective nature and your commitment to His ways. Allow His promise of deliverance to encourage and strengthen you as you navigate life's challenges.

DAY 32

Overcoming Temptation with God's Faithfulness

1 Corinthians 10:13 (NIV)

"No temptation has overtaken you except what is common to mankind. And God is faithful; he will not let you be tempted beyond what you can bear. But when you are tempted, he will also provide a way out so that you can endure it."

Devotional

1 Corinthians 10:13 offers a powerful reassurance for those facing temptation and trials. This verse is a promise of God's faithfulness and His provision in our moments of struggle.

The verse starts with, "No temptation has overtaken you except what is common to mankind." This means that the struggles and temptations we face are not unique to us alone; they are part of the human experience. Recognizing this can provide comfort and perspective, knowing that others have faced similar challenges and have overcome them.

The heart of the promise is found in the declaration, "And God is faithful; he will not let you be tempted beyond what you can bear." God's faithfulness ensures that He will never allow us to be tested beyond our capacity to endure. This means that even in our most challenging moments, we are not abandoned; God's strength and support are always available to help us persevere.

The verse concludes with, "But when you are tempted, he will also provide a way out so that you can endure it." God's provision includes not just the strength to bear temptation but also a way of escape. This promise invites us to actively seek and recognize the paths God provides to overcome temptation, whether through prayer, wise counsel, or other means He places before us.

Understanding this verse encourages us to rely on God's faithfulness and to trust that He will provide the necessary resources and opportunities to overcome our challenges.

Prayer

Heavenly Father,
I thank You for the promise in 1 Corinthians 10:13 that You are faithful and will not allow me to be tempted beyond what I can bear. Help me to trust in Your provision and to seek the way out that You provide. Strengthen me to endure temptation and to recognize Your support in every challenge I face. May Your faithfulness be a constant source of encouragement and strength.
In Jesus' name, Amen.

CONTEMPLATION

Spend a few moments in quiet reflection, focusing on God's faithfulness and His promise to provide a way out of temptation. Allow His assurance to strengthen your resolve and guide you through your struggles.

DAY 33
The Essence of Love

1 Corinthians 13:4-7 (NIV)

"Love is patient, love is kind. It does not envy, it does not boast, it is not proud. It does not dishonor others, it is not self-seeking, it is not easily angered, it keeps no record of wrongs. Love does not delight in evil but rejoices with the truth. It always protects, always trusts, always hopes, always perseveres."

Devotional

In 1 Corinthians 13:4-7, Paul provides us with a beautiful portrait of love—a love that is both profound and practical. This passage is often read at weddings and celebrations, but its call to embody true love extends far beyond these occasions into our daily lives.

PATIENCE AND KINDNESS: Love is patient and kind, traits that demand a selfless approach to our interactions with others. Patience allows us to endure challenges and imperfections in others without frustration, while kindness moves us to act with compassion and generosity.

HUMILITY AND INTEGRITY: Love is not envious, boastful, or proud. It does not seek to elevate oneself at the expense of others but values and honors each individual. Such love rejects dishonor and strives to uplift those around us.

FORGIVENESS AND TRUTH: True love keeps no record of wrongs and does not delight in evil. Instead, it embraces forgiveness and celebrates truth. This means letting go of past grievances and rejoicing in honesty and righteousness.

PROTECTION AND PERSEVERANCE: Love always protects, trusts, hopes, and perseveres. It shields others from harm, believes in their potential, remains hopeful through trials, and endures in the face of difficulties.

Prayer

Heavenly Father,
Thank You for the gift of love, which You have demonstrated through Your Son, Jesus Christ. Help me to embody this kind of love in my daily life. Teach me to be patient and kind, to let go of envy and pride, and to honor others above myself. Fill my heart with forgiveness and guide me to rejoice in truth.

Lord, I ask for Your strength to protect those around me, to trust in Your plans, to hold on to hope, and to persevere through challenges. Let Your love shine through me, reflecting Your grace and mercy.
In Jesus' name, Amen.

CONTEMPLATION

Contemplate the qualities of love described in this passage and reflect on how you can better embody them. Allow God's love to transform your interactions, making you a vessel of His grace and kindness.

DAY 34
The Best Gift

Psalm 84:11 (NIV)

"For the Lord God is a sun and shield; the Lord bestows favor and honor; no good thing does he withhold from those whose walk is blameless."

Devotional

Psalm 84:11 offers a profound reminder of the nature of God's provision and protection. This verse paints a vivid picture of God as both a sun and a shield. As the sun, He provides light, warmth, and life—essential elements for growth and vitality. As a shield, He offers protection, guarding us from harm and shielding us from adversity.

The verse also highlights God's generosity and justice. He bestows favor and honor, not based on our merit but out of His boundless grace. This favor is not a mere earthly reward but a reflection of His divine love and righteousness. God's honor and favor encompass His blessings, guidance, and the assurance of His presence in our lives.

Importantly, Psalm 84:11 assures us that God does not withhold any good thing from those whose walk is blameless. This does not imply perfection but a heart aligned with God's will—a life striving to follow His commands and reflect His character. God's promise is that He will provide for our needs and bless us in ways that are ultimately for our good.

Prayer

Heavenly Father,

Thank You for being my sun and shield. Your light brings clarity to my path, and Your protection surrounds me in times of trouble. I am grateful for Your favor and honor, which You bestow out of Your infinite grace and love.

Help me to walk blamelessly before You, not in perfection, but in sincere devotion and trust. Guide my steps, and let my life reflect Your goodness and truth. I trust that You will not withhold any good thing from me, and I am thankful for Your continuous provision and protection.

Lord, help me to rest in Your promises and to seek Your guidance in all things. May Your presence be my comfort and Your favor my strength.

In Jesus' name, Amen.

CONTEMPLATION

Reflect on the ways God has been a sun and shield in your life. Contemplate His favor and the good things He has provided. Allow His promises to deepen your trust and strengthen your walk with Him.

DAY 35
The Lord's Compassionate Care

Psalm 146:9 (NIV)

*"The Lord watches over the foreigner and sustains the fatherless and the widow,
but he frustrates the ways of the wicked."*

Devotional

Psalm 146:9 provides a powerful depiction of God's heart for the vulnerable and marginalized. In this verse, the psalmist highlights three key groups: the foreigner, the fatherless, and the widow—those who often face societal neglect and hardship. The Lord's care for these individuals underscores His deep compassion and justice.

GOD WATCHES OVER THE FOREIGNER: The foreigner, or stranger, represents those who are away from their homeland and might feel isolated or unprotected. God's vigilance assures that they are not overlooked or abandoned. He extends His care to those who are in unfamiliar surroundings, reminding us that His love transcends boundaries and embraces all people.

SUSTAINING THE FATHERLESS AND THE WIDOW: The fatherless and the widow symbolize those who lack the support and protection typically provided by family. In a time when these individuals are particularly vulnerable, God promises to sustain them, providing their needs and offering a sense of security and hope. His provision extends beyond material needs, encompassing emotional and spiritual support.

FRUSTRATING THE WAYS OF THE WICKED: In contrast, God frustrates the ways of the wicked—those who act unjustly or harm others. His justice ensures that wrongdoing does not go unchecked, and that the oppressed are not forgotten.

Prayer

Heavenly Father,
Thank You for Your steadfast care and protection over those who are vulnerable and in need. I am grateful for Your promise to watch over the foreigner, sustain the fatherless and the widow, and bring justice against the wicked.

Help me to mirror Your compassion in my own life. Open my eyes to the needs of those around me and give me the courage to offer support and kindness. Teach me to be an instrument of Your justice and mercy, reflecting Your love in tangible ways. Lord, I trust in Your righteous ways and ask for Your guidance to live in a manner that honors You. May Your care for the vulnerable inspire my actions and deepen my commitment to serve others with Your love.
In Jesus' name, Amen.

CONTEMPLATION

Reflect on how God has been a source of comfort and support in your own life. Consider how you can extend that same care to those in need, embodying His love and justice in your daily actions.

DAY 36
Embracing God's Deliverance

Psalm 116:6 (NIV)
"The Lord protects the unwary; when I was brought low, he saved me."

Devotional

Psalm 116:6 offers a comforting assurance of God's protective and saving power. The verse speaks to both the tender care and the mighty deliverance that God provides. It highlights two profound aspects of God's relationship with His people: His protection for the unwary and His salvation in times of distress.

PROTECTION FOR THE UNWARY: The term "unwary" refers to those who may be caught off guard or unaware of impending dangers. It signifies vulnerability and a lack of foresight. Yet, the verse reassures us that God watches over those who find themselves in these situations. His protection is not limited to those who are vigilant but extends to all who are in need, even if they are unaware of the threats around them.

DELIVERANCE IN TIMES OF DISTRESS: The latter part of the verse recounts a personal testimony of being "brought low" and experiencing God's saving intervention. This low point could be a moment of physical, emotional, or spiritual struggle. The promise here is that when we are at our lowest, God is present to lift us up and rescue us. His deliverance is not just a momentary relief but a profound act of saving grace that restores and renews.

Prayer

Heavenly Father,
Thank You for Your unwavering protection and for being my refuge in times of distress. I am grateful for Your care, even when I am unaware of the dangers around me. You are my shield and my deliverer.

In moments when I feel brought low or overwhelmed, remind me of Your saving power. Help me to trust in Your provision and to lean on You for strength and comfort. May I find solace in knowing that You are always with me, ready to lift me up and guide me through.
Lord, teach me to reflect Your protection and care in my interactions with others. Let my life be a testament to Your goodness and faithfulness.
In Jesus' name, I pray. Amen.

CONTEMPLATION

Contemplate the ways in which God has protected and delivered you. Reflect on His care in your times of need and allow this realization to deepen your trust and gratitude.

DAY 37
More Than Conquerors Through Christ

Romans 8:37 (NIV)
"No, in all these things we are more than conquerors through him who loved us."

Devotional

Romans 8:37 is a powerful declaration of victory and assurance in our walk with Christ. The Apostle Paul, inspired by the Holy Spirit, reminds us that despite the trials and adversities we face, we are "more than conquerors" through Jesus Christ. This verse is not just a comforting thought but a profound truth that speaks to the transformative power of God's love and grace.

MORE THAN CONQUERORS: To be "more than conquerors" means that our victory is not only about overcoming obstacles but also about triumphing with an overwhelming sense of assurance and completeness. Conquering implies defeating a challenge, but being "more than conquerors" means our victory is secured and abundant. It signifies that our struggles and hardships do not define us, but rather our identity is found in Christ's ultimate triumph over sin and death.

THROUGH HIM WHO LOVED US: The source of our victory is not found in our own strength or abilities but in Jesus Christ, who loves us deeply. His love is the foundation of our conquering power. It is through His sacrifice and resurrection that we gain victory over sin and find the strength to endure life's trials. This love is a constant, unchanging force that equips us to face challenges with confidence.

Prayer

Heavenly Father,
Thank You for the incredible victory we have through Jesus Christ. I am grateful for Your love that empowers us to be more than conquerors, no matter what challenges we face. Help me to fully embrace this truth and to walk in the assurance of Your unending love.

When I encounter difficulties or feel overwhelmed, remind me of the victory secured by Christ. Strengthen my faith and help me to live boldly, knowing that Your love and power are greater than any struggle I may face.

Lord, let Your victory shine through me, and may my life reflect the triumph and assurance found in Christ.
In Jesus' name, I pray. Amen.

CONTEMPLATION

Reflect on the victories you have experienced through Christ and the strength that His love provides. Let this awareness shape your approach to current and future challenges, knowing that you are more than a conqueror through Him.

DAY 38
The Crown of Glory

1 Peter 5:4 (NIV)

"And when the Chief Shepherd appears, you will receive the crown of glory that will never fade away."

Devotional

1 Peter 5:4 offers a profound promise of reward and encouragement for those who faithfully serve and lead in their spiritual journey. The verse speaks to the ultimate recognition and reward that believers will receive when Jesus, the Chief Shepherd, returns. It's a reminder of the eternal glory that awaits those who have followed Christ faithfully.

THE CHIEF SHEPHERD: The title "Chief Shepherd" emphasizes Christ's supreme authority and care over His flock. Just as a shepherd guides, protects, and nurtures the sheep, Jesus, as the Chief Shepherd, is the ultimate leader and caretaker of His people. His return is not just a future event but a profound moment of fulfillment and reward.

THE CROWN OF GLORY: The promise of a "crown of glory" symbolizes the honor and reward given by Christ. Unlike earthly crowns, which are temporary and subject to decay, this crown is eternal and imperishable. It represents not only recognition for faithful service but also the everlasting beauty and joy of being in Christ's presence. This crown is a testament to the divine approval and everlasting reward for those who have lived with integrity and dedication.

Prayer

Heavenly Father,

Thank You for the promise of the crown of glory that awaits those who faithfully follow and serve You. I am grateful for Your assurance that our labor is not in vain and that You will reward those who remain steadfast in their faith.

Help me to live each day with a heart committed to Your service, knowing that my efforts are seen and valued by You. Strengthen my resolve to persevere in my walk with You, and let the hope of eternal glory inspire me to serve with joy and dedication.

Lord, may I reflect Your love and grace in all I do, and may I look forward with anticipation to the day when I receive the crown of glory from You, my Chief Shepherd.
In Jesus' name, I pray. Amen.

CONTEMPLATION

Reflect on how you can remain faithful and dedicated in your service to God, trusting in His promise of eternal reward. Let the hope of the crown of glory inspire and encourage you in your daily walk with Christ.

DAY 39
The Radiance of the Righteous

Matthew 13:43 (NIV)
"Then the righteous will shine like the sun in the kingdom of their Father.
Whoever has ears, let them hear."

Devotional

In Matthew 13:43, Jesus offers a vivid and encouraging vision of the future for those who live righteously. This verse paints a picture of ultimate reward and transformation: the righteous will shine like the sun in the kingdom of their Father. It's a promise of divine recognition and the fulfillment of God's promises.

SHINING LIKE THE SUN: To 'shine like the sun' is a powerful metaphor. The sun represents brilliance, warmth, and life-giving energy. When Jesus says the righteous will shine like the sun, He is describing the radiance of their transformed lives in His kingdom. This imagery suggests not only an external splendor but an inner purity and joy that emanate from a life lived in accordance with God's will. The brightness symbolizes the true nature of righteousness, which reflects God's glory and serves as a beacon of hope and truth to others.

IN THE KINGDOM OF THEIR FATHER: This promise is anchored in the reality of God's eternal kingdom. The "kingdom of their Father" represents the ultimate fulfillment of God's plan—a place where righteousness reigns and where believers experience complete communion with God. It is in this divine kingdom that the full glory of the righteous will be revealed.

Prayer

Heavenly Father,
Thank You for the promise that those who live righteously will shine like the sun in Your kingdom. I am grateful for the hope and assurance that my efforts to live according to Your will are recognized and valued.

Help me to reflect Your light in all that I do, living in a way that honors You and shines Your love and truth to those around me. May my life be a testament to Your grace and righteousness, and may I look forward with anticipation to the day when Your kingdom is fully realized.

Lord, grant me the strength to persevere in my faith and to shine brightly in Your name.
In Jesus' name, I pray. Amen.

CONTEMPLATION

Reflect on how you can let your life shine with the light of Christ. Consider the ways you can embody His righteousness and be a beacon of hope and truth in your daily interactions.

DAY 40
The Faithfulness of God

Joshua 23:14 (NIV)
"Now I am about to go the way of all the earth. You know with all your heart and soul that not one of all the good promises the Lord your God gave you has failed. Every promise has been fulfilled; not one has failed."

Devotional

In Joshua 23:14, as Joshua nears the end of his life, he provides a powerful testament to the faithfulness of God. He recounts with assurance that every promise God made to the Israelites has been fulfilled. This declaration is more than a historical account; it serves as a profound reminder of God's unwavering reliability and the fulfillment of His word.

THE CERTAINTY OF GOD'S PROMISES: Joshua's words underscore a central truth of the Christian faith: God is faithful to His promises. Throughout the Israelites' journey, from their liberation from Egypt to their settlement in the Promised Land, God's promises were steadfast. Even when challenges and doubts arose, His word proved true. Joshua's testimony is a reminder that God's promises are not contingent on our circumstances but are secure in His unchanging nature.

FULFILLMENT AND ASSURANCE: Reflecting on the complete fulfillment of God's promises offers assurance and hope. Just as Joshua witnessed every promise come to pass, we can trust that God will be faithful to His promises in our own lives. Whether it's promises of provision, guidance, or eternal life, we can have confidence that what God has spoken will be realized. This confidence is not just for grand promises but also for the daily assurances of His presence and care.

Prayer

Heavenly Father,
Thank You for Your faithfulness and for fulfilling every promise You have made. I am grateful for the assurance that Your word is true and that You are a reliable and trustworthy God.

Help me to remember Your promises and to trust in Your timing and provision. Strengthen my faith and encourage me to rely on Your promises in every circumstance. May I find comfort and confidence in knowing that You are faithful to complete what You have started in my life.

Lord, as I navigate my journey, let Your promises be a guiding light and a source of hope.
In Jesus' name, I pray. Amen.

CONTEMPLATION

Contemplate the ways in which God's promises have been fulfilled in your life. Reflect on the assurance this brings and how you can trust Him more deeply in your current circumstances.

DAY 41
Purpose and Promise

Jeremiah 1:5 (NIV)
"Before I formed you in the womb I knew you, before you were born I set you apart; I appointed you as a prophet to the nations."

Devotional

Jeremiah 1:5 is a profound declaration of God's intimate knowledge and sovereign purpose for each person. This verse captures the essence of divine foreknowledge and calling, offering deep encouragement and insight into God's relationship with us.

INTIMATE KNOWLEDGE: God's statement, "Before I formed you in the womb I knew you," reveals His intimate and personal knowledge of each of us long before our physical existence. This divine awareness is not distant or abstract; it is deeply personal. God's knowledge of us encompasses our strengths, weaknesses, dreams, and struggles. It assures us that we are not merely products of chance but are intricately known and valued by our Creator.

PURPOSE AND CALLING: The next part of the verse, "Before you were born I set you apart," speaks to the unique purpose God has for each life. Even before our birth, God has a plan and calling for us. This setting apart signifies that our lives have meaning and direction that align with His greater purpose. For Jeremiah, this calling was to be a prophet to the nations, but for each of us, God has a specific and significant role that reflects His plan for our lives.

Prayer

Heavenly Father,
Thank You for Your intimate knowledge of me and for the purpose You have designed for my life. I am grateful that even before I was born, You knew me and set me apart for a unique calling.

Help me to embrace the truth that I am created with intention and purpose. Guide me in discovering and fulfilling the role You have set for me. When I face doubts or uncertainties, remind me of Your personal and loving plan for my life.

Lord, may I walk confidently in the calling You have given me, knowing that I am known and valued by You.
In Jesus' name, I pray. Amen.

CONTEMPLATION

Spend a few moments in quiet reflection, focusing on the truth of God's intimate knowledge and purposeful plans for you. Allow this assurance to strengthen your faith and guide you as you seek to live out your calling.

DAY 42
Restored and Forgiven

Isaiah 44:22 (NIV)
"I have swept away your offenses like a cloud, your sins like the morning mist. Return to me, for I have redeemed you."

Devotional

Isaiah 44:22 is a powerful message of redemption and forgiveness, offering a beautiful image of God's grace. This verse provides profound comfort, especially for those who are burdened by guilt or sin. It captures the essence of divine forgiveness and the invitation to return to God.

SWEPT AWAY LIKE A CLOUD: The imagery of offenses being "swept away like a cloud" evokes a sense of complete removal and liberation. Just as clouds disperse and vanish, so does God remove our sins from us. This picture illustrates how God's forgiveness is not partial or temporary but thorough and all-encompassing. It emphasizes that our past offenses are not held against us but are removed completely.

SINS LIKE THE MORNING MIST: The comparison of sins to the "morning mist" further reinforces this idea of total erasure. Just as the mist dissipates with the rising sun, our sins are dissolved in the light of God's grace. This imagery assures us that no matter how persistent our guilt may feel, God's forgiveness is more powerful and enduring.

DAY 42
Restored and Forgiven

Isaiah 44:22 (NIV)
"I have swept away your offenses like a cloud, your sins like the morning mist. Return to me, for I have redeemed you."

Devotional

Isaiah 44:22 is a powerful message of redemption and forgiveness, offering a beautiful image of God's grace. This verse provides profound comfort, especially for those who are burdened by guilt or sin. It captures the essence of divine forgiveness and the invitation to return to God.

SWEPT AWAY LIKE A CLOUD: The imagery of offenses being "swept away like a cloud" evokes a sense of complete removal and liberation. Just as clouds disperse and vanish, so does God remove our sins from us. This picture illustrates how God's forgiveness is not partial or temporary but thorough and all-encompassing. It emphasizes that our past offenses are not held against us but are removed completely.

SINS LIKE THE MORNING MIST: The comparison of sins to the "morning mist" further reinforces this idea of total erasure. Just as the mist dissipates with the rising sun, our sins are dissolved in the light of God's grace. This imagery assures us that no matter how persistent our guilt may feel, God's forgiveness is more powerful and enduring.

INVITATION TO RETURN: God's call to "Return to me" is a gracious invitation to reconciliation and renewal. Despite our failures and shortcomings, God's arms are open, ready to welcome us back. This invitation is not just for a one-time return but a continual process of drawing near to God, experiencing His redemption daily.

Prayer

Heavenly Father,
Thank You for the incredible gift of Your forgiveness and for
sweeping away my offenses and sins. I am deeply grateful for
Your grace, which removes my guilt and allows me to start
anew.

Help me to fully embrace Your forgiveness and to return to You
with a sincere heart. Let me live in the light of Your redemption,
free from the burden of past mistakes. Guide me in walking
closely with You, knowing that Your grace is sufficient and
everlasting.

Lord, may Your love and forgiveness inspire me to reflect Your
grace to others, sharing the hope and renewal found in You.
In Jesus' name, I pray. Amen.

CONTEMPLATION

Contemplate the depth of God's forgiveness in your life.
Reflect on how His grace has removed your sins and
how you can respond to His invitation with a heart of
gratitude and renewal.

DAY 43
A Beloved Father's Promise

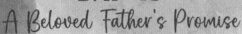
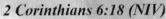

2 Corinthians 6:18 (NIV)
"I will be a Father to you, and you will be my sons and daughters, says the Lord Almighty."

Devotional

2 Corinthians 6:18 is a profound declaration of God's commitment and relational promise to His people. In this verse, the Apostle Paul, quoting from the Old Testament, emphasizes the intimate and personal relationship that God desires to have with us. This promise speaks to the heart of our identity and our place within God's family.

"I will be a Father to you" is a powerful affirmation of God's role as our Heavenly Father. It conveys not just a distant or formal relationship but a close, caring, and nurturing presence. God's fatherhood is characterized by His love, guidance, and provision. Unlike earthly fathers who may falter, God's fatherly care is perfect and unfailing. This promise assures us of His constant support and protection.

"You will be my sons and daughters" reinforces our identity as part of God's family. This familial language highlights the warmth and closeness of our relationship with Him. It signifies not only acceptance but a deep, enduring connection. Being called God's sons and daughters means we are heirs to His promises and recipients of His love and grace.

"says the Lord Almighty" underscores the authority and certainty of this promise. The title "Lord Almighty" reflects God's supreme power and sovereignty, affirming that His promises are secure and reliable. It is not a conditional or temporary assurance but a firm, eternal truth.

Prayer

Heavenly Father,
Thank You for the promise in 2 Corinthians 6:18 that You will be a Father to me and that I am Your beloved son/daughter. I am grateful for Your constant love, guidance, and provision. Help me to fully embrace my identity as part of Your family and to live with confidence in Your care. May Your fatherly presence bring comfort and strength to my life. Guide me to share this promise of Your love with others, reflecting Your warmth and grace. In Jesus' name, Amen.

CONTEMPLATION

Spend a few moments in quiet reflection, focusing on the depth of God's fatherly love and the security of being His child. Allow this truth to fill you with peace and confidence as you experience His care and guidance.

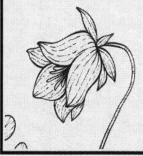

DAY 44
Guidance and Assurance

Psalm 32:8 (NIV)
"I will instruct you and teach you in the way you should go; I will counsel you with my loving eye on you."

Devotional

Psalm 32:8 is a comforting promise from God that highlights His desire to guide and counsel us with His unwavering love and attention. This verse is a beautiful assurance of God's personal involvement in our lives, offering us direction and support as we navigate our journey.

The verse begins with, "I will instruct you and teach you in the way you should go." This promise reflects God's commitment to providing us with wisdom and direction. Just as a teacher guides a student through their learning, God offers us instruction and guidance for the path we should take. Whether we are making decisions, facing challenges, or seeking purpose, God's guidance is available to us, helping us to follow the right path.

The latter part of the verse, "I will counsel you with my loving eye on you," adds a layer of deep personal care. The image of God's "loving eye" conveys His attentive and compassionate oversight. It's not just that God gives us directions and then leaves us to figure things out on our own: rather, He watches over us with love, offering continuous counsel and support. This assures us that we are never alone in our journey and that God's guidance is paired with His constant care.

Psalm 32:8 encourages us to trust in God's guidance and to rely on His loving oversight. It invites us to seek His counsel in all aspects of our lives, knowing that His instruction is both wise and filled with love.

Prayer

Heavenly Father,

Thank You for the promise in Psalm 32:8 that You will instruct and teach me in the way I should go. I am grateful for Your loving eye that watches over me and offers counsel with compassion. Help me to seek Your guidance in all areas of my life and to trust in Your care as I follow the path You have set before me. May I feel Your presence and assurance in every step I take, knowing that You are always with me.

In Jesus' name, Amen.

CONTEMPLATION

Spend a few moments in quiet reflection, focusing on the assurance of God's guidance and loving care. Allow this promise to bring peace and confidence as you seek His direction and walk in His ways.

DAY 45
Trusting God's Guidance

Proverbs 3:5-6 (NIV)
"Trust in the Lord with all your heart and lean not on your own understanding; in all your ways submit to him, and he will make your paths straight."

Devotional

Proverbs 3:5-6 offers a profound invitation to trust in God's guidance and wisdom. These verses encapsulate a fundamental principle of the Christian faith: surrendering our own understanding and relying wholly on God's direction.

"Trust in the Lord with all your heart" begins with a call to wholehearted trust. Trusting God is not a partial or half-hearted endeavor; it requires a full commitment of our hearts and minds. To trust God means to place our complete confidence in His ability to lead us and to act in our best interests, even when circumstances are unclear or challenging.

"Lean not on your own understanding" encourages us to move beyond our limited human perspective. While our reasoning and experiences are valuable, they are often incomplete and fallible. By acknowledging that our understanding is imperfect, we open ourselves to receiving God's perfect wisdom and guidance.

"In all your ways submit to him" calls us to integrate God's guidance into every aspect of our lives. This means seeking His direction in both the significant and everyday matters, trusting that His way is better than our own.

"And he will make your paths straight" concludes with a promise of clarity and direction. God assures us that when we trust Him and submit to His guidance, He will lead us in the right direction. This "straight path" symbolizes a journey that is not only clear but also aligned with His purposes and full of His blessings.

Prayer

Heavenly Father,
I thank You for the promise in Proverbs 3:5-6 that You will guide
me when I trust in You with all my heart and submit to Your
will. Help me to lean not on my own understanding but to seek
Your wisdom in every area of my life. Grant me the faith to trust
Your direction and the humility to submit to Your guidance. May
I experience the clarity and blessing of walking in the path You
have set before me
In Jesus' name, Amen.

CONTEMPLATION

Spend a few moments in quiet reflection, focusing on
areas where you need to trust God more fully. Allow
the assurance of His guidance to bring peace and
confidence as you seek to follow His straight path.

DAY 46
Committing Our Work to the Lord

Proverbs 16:3 (NIV)
"Commit to the Lord whatever you do, and he will establish your plans."

Devotional

Proverbs 16:3 is a powerful reminder of the importance of dedicating all our endeavors to God. This verse offers encouragement and assurance that when we align our efforts with God's will, He will support and establish our plans.

"Commit to the Lord whatever you do" is an invitation to bring every aspect of our lives under God's care and direction. To commit means to entrust something to someone with full confidence. In this context, it means dedicating our work, goals, and daily activities to God. Whether we are starting a new project, making important decisions, or simply going about our daily routines, this verse encourages us to invite God into every part of our lives.

The promise that "He will establish your plans" follows as a reassuring outcome of our commitment. When we place our trust in God and seek His guidance, He promises to establish and bless our efforts. This doesn't necessarily mean that every plan will unfold exactly as we envision, but it does mean that God will guide and direct us in ways that align with His greater purposes for our lives. His establishment of our plans includes His wisdom and timing, ensuring that our efforts are fruitful and aligned with His will.

This verse calls us to live with intentionality, recognizing that our work and decisions are most effective when guided by God. It encourages us to pray over our plans, seek His counsel, and trust that He will bring about what is best for us according to His perfect will.

Prayer

Heavenly Father,
I thank You for the promise in Proverbs 16:3 that You will establish the plans I commit to You. Help me to dedicate every aspect of my life to You, trusting that You will guide and bless my efforts. Give me wisdom to seek Your will and patience to wait for Your perfect timing. May my work and decisions reflect Your purpose and bring glory to Your name.
In Jesus' name, Amen.

CONTEMPLATION

Spend a few moments in quiet reflection, considering the plans and goals you currently have. Commit these to God, asking for His guidance and blessing. Trust in His promise to establish and direct your efforts according to His will.

DAY 47
Contentment in God's Presence

Hebrews 13:5 (NIV)
"Keep your lives free from the love of money and be content with what you have, because God has said, 'Never will I leave you; never will I forsake you.'"

Devotional

Hebrews 13:5 offers a profound promise that speaks directly to our deepest fears and longings. In a world that often equates success and security with material wealth, this verse reminds us of the true source of our contentment and stability—God's unwavering presence.

"Keep your lives free from the love of money" challenges us to reassess our priorities and values. Money and material possessions can easily become the focus of our lives, leading us to seek security and happiness in temporary and uncertain things. This verse calls us to shift our focus from the pursuit of wealth to a deeper reliance on God, who provides all our needs.

"Be content with what you have" encourages us to cultivate a heart of gratitude and satisfaction. Contentment is not about having everything we want but finding peace and joy in what we already have. It's a mindset that trusts in God's provision and is rooted in the understanding that true fulfillment comes from Him, not from accumulating more.

The verse concludes with a powerful reassurance: "because God has said, 'Never will I leave you; never will I forsake you.'" This promise is a cornerstone of our faith. It affirms that regardless of our circumstances, God's presence is constant and His faithfulness is unshakeable. When we face challenges or uncertainties, we can take comfort in knowing that God is with us, never abandoning us or leaving us without support.

Prayer

Heavenly Father,

Thank You for the promise in Hebrews 13:5 that You will never leave me or forsake me. Help me to keep my life free from the love of money and to find contentment in what I have. Teach me to trust in Your constant presence and provision, regardless of my circumstances. May I always remember that true security and fulfillment come from You alone.

In Jesus' name, Amen.

CONTEMPLATION

Spend a few moments in quiet reflection, focusing on God's promise of His unwavering presence. Allow this assurance to bring peace and contentment as you release worries about material things and embrace the fullness of God's provision.

DAY 48
Embracing the Promise of God

Acts 2:39 (NIV)

"The promise is for you and your children and for all who are far off—for all whom the Lord our God will call."

Devotional

Acts 2:39 is a beautiful declaration of the inclusiveness and far-reaching nature of God's promises. This verse is part of Peter's sermon on the day of Pentecost, where he addresses the crowd about the gift of the Holy Spirit and the promise of salvation.

"The promise is for you and your children" emphasizes that God's promises are not limited by age or generation. The message of salvation and the gift of the Holy Spirit are offered to everyone, from the youngest to the oldest. It reflects God's desire for a multi-generational relationship with His people, ensuring that His promises are passed down and experienced across generations.

"And for all who are far off" extends this promise beyond the immediate context to include those who are distant, whether geographically, spiritually, or emotionally. No matter where we find ourselves—whether we feel distant from God, or are struggling with doubt—this promise assures us that God's reach is vast and His invitation is open to all.

"For all whom the Lord our God will call" underscores the inclusivity of God's invitation. It's not based on our merits or proximity but on God's sovereign choice and calling. Everyone whom God calls is welcomed into His promise, demonstrating His grace and love.

Prayer

Heavenly Father,
I thank You for the promise in Acts 2:39 that Your salvation and the gift of the Holy Spirit are for me, my children, and all whom You call. I am grateful for Your inclusive love and grace that reaches across generations and distances. Help me to embrace Your promises in my life and to share this hope with others. Guide me to respond faithfully to Your call and to trust in Your ever-present and loving invitation.
In Jesus' name, Amen.

CONTEMPLATION

Spend a few moments in quiet reflection, considering the breadth and depth of God's promise. Allow this assurance to fill you with hope and confidence, as you embrace His invitation and share it with those around you.

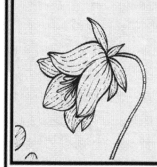

DAY 49
Finding Peace in God's Presence

2 Thessalonians 3:16 (NIV)
"Now may the Lord of peace himself give you peace at all times and in every way. The Lord be with all of you."

Devotional

2 Thessalonians 3:16 offers a profound blessing from the Apostle Paul, capturing the essence of God's promise to grant us peace in every circumstance. As Paul concludes his letter to the Thessalonians, he emphasizes the peace that comes from the Lord, inviting us to experience this peace in our own lives.

"Now may the Lord of peace himself" starts with an acknowledgment of God's nature as the source of peace. God is not just a giver of peace; He is the very essence of peace. This means that true and lasting peace comes from a relationship with Him. He is the foundation upon which all our peace is built.

"Give you peace at all times and in every way" extends this promise to every aspect of our lives. Whether we are experiencing calm or chaos, joy or struggle, God's peace is available to us. This peace is not contingent on our circumstances but is a deep, inner tranquility that sustains us through every trial and triumph. It is a peace that surpasses understanding, guarding our hearts and minds (Philippians 4:7).

"The Lord be with all of you" is a reminder of God's continuous presence in our lives. It's not just that He gives us peace, but He is with us at all times. His presence is a constant source of comfort and strength, assuring us that we are never alone, regardless of our circumstances.

Prayer

Heavenly Father,

I thank You for the promise of peace found in 2 Thessalonians 3:16. I am grateful that You are the Lord of peace and that You offer me Your peace at all times and in every way. Help me to experience Your peace deeply and to trust in Your constant presence. May Your peace guard my heart and mind, and may I reflect this peace to those around me.

In Jesus' name, Amen.

CONTEMPLATION

Spend a few moments in quiet reflection, focusing on the peace that God offers. Allow His presence to soothe your soul and fill you with a deep sense of calm, regardless of your current circumstances.

DAY 50
Assurance in Times of Trouble

Psalm 91:15 (NIV)
"He will call on me, and I will answer him; I will be with him in trouble, I will deliver him and honor him."

Devotional

Psalm 91:15 is a powerful promise from God that provides comfort and assurance during times of difficulty and distress. This verse highlights God's commitment to respond to our calls for help, His presence in our troubles, and His deliverance and honor.

"He will call on me, and I will answer him" starts with the assurance that God is always available to hear our cries. In moments of trouble, God invites us to reach out to Him. He is not distant or indifferent; rather, He is attentive and ready to respond to our prayers. This promise reminds us that no matter how dire our circumstances may seem, we are never alone. God is just a call away, and He promises to answer us when we seek Him.

"I will be with him in trouble" emphasizes God's unwavering presence. He does not promise to remove us from all trouble but assures us that He will be with us through it. This presence provides comfort and strength, knowing that we are not facing our challenges on our own. God's companionship in our difficulties reassures us that He is guiding and supporting us every step of the way.

"I will deliver him and honor him" concludes with the promise of deliverance and honor. God is committed to rescuing us from our troubles and providing a way through them. Additionally, He promises to honor us, which can be understood as His acknowledgment and reward for our faithfulness and trust in Him. God's deliverance often comes in ways we may not expect, but His intention is always for our ultimate good.

Prayer

Heavenly Father,

Thank You for the promise in Psalm 91:15 that You will answer me when I call, be with me in trouble, deliver me, and honor me. I am grateful for Your constant presence and support in my times of need. Help me to trust in Your deliverance and to remain faithful, knowing that You are always working for my good. May I find comfort and strength in Your promises and reflect Your faithfulness in my life.

In Jesus' name, Amen.

CONTEMPLATION

Spend a few moments in quiet reflection, considering the times when you have called on God and experienced His response. Allow this assurance to bring you peace and confidence as you face any current or future challenges.

DAY 51
Anticipating God's Blessings

Isaiah 64:4 (NIV)

"Since ancient times no one has heard, no ear has perceived, no eye has seen any God besides you, who acts on behalf of those who wait for him."

Devotional

Isaiah 64:4 is a beautiful reminder of God's unique nature and His profound commitment to those who trust in Him. This verse highlights God's unmatched greatness and His faithful actions toward those who eagerly await His intervention.

"Since ancient times no one has heard, no ear has perceived, no eye has seen any God besides you" speaks to the incomparable nature of God. He is unparalleled in His power and goodness. Throughout history, no one has witnessed a god like our God—one who is deeply involved in the lives of His people and acts on their behalf. This verse underscores the exclusivity of God's character and His unique role as a loving and attentive Creator.

"Who acts on behalf of those who wait for him" offers a powerful promise. God is not a distant deity but one who is actively involved in the lives of those who wait upon Him. Waiting on God means placing our trust and hope in Him, anticipating His actions and timing. It involves patience and faith, trusting that God's ways are perfect and His timing is impeccable. God promises to act on behalf of those who trust Him, ensuring that our needs and desires are met according to His perfect plan.

This verse encourages us to maintain a posture of expectancy and trust. While waiting on God can sometimes be challenging, we are assured that He is working behind the scenes, preparing blessings and answers that are beyond our imagination. Our waiting is not in vain but is a part of God's larger plan to work for our good.

Prayer

Heavenly Father,

I thank You for the promise in Isaiah 64:4 that You act on behalf of those who wait for You. I am in awe of Your unique nature and unmatched greatness. Help me to trust in Your perfect timing and to wait with patience and expectancy. Remind me of Your past faithfulness and give me confidence that You are working on my behalf, even when I cannot see it. I place my hope in You and look forward to the blessings You have prepared for me.

In Jesus' name, Amen.

CONTEMPLATION

Spend a few moments in quiet reflection, considering the ways God has acted on your behalf in the past. Allow this reflection to build your trust and patience as you wait for His future blessings.

DAY 52
Trusting Our Shepherd

Psalm 23:1 (NIV)
"The Lord is my shepherd, I lack nothing."

Devotional

Psalm 23:1 is a profound statement of trust and assurance, encapsulating the essence of God's role in our lives as our Shepherd. This verse, the opening line of one of the most beloved psalms, assures us of God's provision and care.

"The Lord is my shepherd" establishes a powerful metaphor for God's relationship with His people. As a shepherd leads, guides, and cares for his sheep, so does the Lord guide and care for us. The shepherd's role includes providing for the sheep's needs, leading them to green pastures and still waters, and protecting them from harm. This imagery reflects God's commitment to nurturing and guiding us through every aspect of our lives.

"I lack nothing" is a declaration of contentment and trust in God's provision. When we acknowledge God as our Shepherd, we recognize that He is fully capable of meeting all our needs. This promise is not just about material provision but encompasses emotional, spiritual, and relational needs as well. It reassures us that God knows what we need even before we ask and that He will provide in His perfect way and timing.

This verse invites us to place our full trust in God's guidance and provision. It encourages us to lean into His care and to find contentment in His ability to meet our needs. Trusting God as our Shepherd means surrendering our anxieties and fears, confident that He is taking care of us and leading us toward what is best.

Prayer

Heavenly Father,

Thank You for being my Shepherd and for the assurance that I lack nothing because of Your provision. I am grateful for Your guidance, care, and protection in my life. Help me to trust You fully, releasing my worries and finding contentment in Your ability to meet all my needs. Teach me to rely on Your leading and to rest in the confidence that You are always with me. In Jesus' name, Amen.

CONTEMPLATION

Spend a few moments in quiet reflection, focusing on the ways God has acted as your Shepherd. Allow His presence and provision to fill you with peace and gratitude, deepening your trust in His care.

DAY 53
Secure in God's Hand

John 10:29 (NIV)
"My Father, who has given them to me, is greater than all; no one can snatch them out of my Father's hand."

Devotional

John 10:29 offers a profound sense of security and reassurance for every believer. In this verse, Jesus speaks of the unbreakable bond between Himself, the Father, and His followers. It emphasizes the immense power of God to protect and keep His people safe.

"My Father, who has given them to me" highlights the relationship between Jesus and God the Father. It reminds us that believers are entrusted into Jesus' care by God Himself. This relationship is built on trust and divine intention, and it signifies a deep, personal connection between the Father, the Son, and us. The Father's gift of believers to Jesus demonstrates His love and commitment to our well-being.

"Is greater than all" asserts the supreme authority and power of God. No one and nothing is greater than God, which means His ability to protect and preserve is unmatched. This power assures us that nothing in the universe can overcome His will or challenge His protection.

"No one can snatch them out of my Father's hand" is a powerful statement of security. It promises that once we are in God's care, we are secure from any threat or harm. This divine protection is absolute and unwavering. No external force, no matter how powerful, can remove us from the safety of God's hand. It provides a profound sense of peace and stability, knowing that our salvation and security are not dependent on our own strength but on God's omnipotent grip.

Prayer

Heavenly Father,
I thank You for the promise in John 10:29 that no one can snatch me out of Your hand. I am grateful for Your supreme power and the security it brings to my life. Help me to rest in the assurance of Your protection and to trust in Your unchanging care. May I find peace in knowing that I am secure in Your hand, regardless of the challenges I face.
In Jesus' name, Amen.

CONTEMPLATION

Spend a few moments in quiet reflection, focusing on the safety and security you have in God's hands. Allow this assurance to fill you with peace and confidence, knowing that you are eternally held and protected by His power.

DAY 54
Healing in the Comfort of God

Psalm 147:3 (NIV)
"He heals the brokenhearted and binds up their wounds."

Devotional

Psalm 147:3 is a verse filled with comfort and hope for those experiencing emotional pain and brokenness. It speaks to the tender care and healing touch of God, who addresses our deepest wounds with compassion and restoration.

"He heals the brokenhearted" begins with a profound promise: God's heart is for those who are hurting. The term "brokenhearted" conveys a sense of deep emotional pain, whether from loss, disappointment, or sorrow. This verse assures us that God is intimately aware of our suffering and is committed to healing our hearts. He does not ignore our pain or leave us to fend for ourselves but actively engages in mending our brokenness.

"And binds up their wounds" further emphasizes God's healing work. The image of binding up wounds portrays God as a skilled and caring healer who tends to our injuries with great attention. Just as a physician carefully dresses a wound to promote healing, God attends to our emotional and spiritual wounds with precision and care. His healing is thorough and restorative, addressing not just the surface but the deeper sources of our distress.

This verse invites us to seek God's comfort and healing when we are struggling. It encourages us to bring our brokenness to Him, trusting that He will not only soothe our pain but also bring about a profound restoration. In God's presence, we find healing for our hearts and a balm for our wounds.

Prayer

Heavenly Father,
I am grateful for the promise in Psalm 147:3 that You heal the brokenhearted and bind up their wounds. I bring my pain and sorrow before You, asking for Your healing touch. Comfort me in my brokenness and restore my heart. Help me to trust in Your care and to find peace in Your presence. I also lift up those around me who are hurting, asking that You bring them the same healing and comfort.
In Jesus' name, Amen.

CONTEMPLATION

Spend a few moments in quiet reflection, inviting God's healing presence into your heart. Allow His comfort to surround you and bring peace, trusting in His ability to mend even the deepest wounds.

DAY 55
Embracing Freedom in Christ

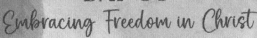

2 Corinthians 3:17 (NIV)
"Now the Lord is the Spirit, and where the Spirit of the Lord is, there is freedom."

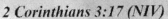

Devotional

2 Corinthians 3:17 is a profound verse that speaks to the transformative power of the Holy Spirit and the freedom that comes from living under His influence. This verse highlights the connection between the presence of the Lord's Spirit and the liberation that believers experience.

"Now the Lord is the Spirit" establishes the divine nature of the Holy Spirit. It reminds us that the Spirit is not merely a force but is indeed the Lord Himself, actively working in our lives. The Spirit is integral to our relationship with God and plays a crucial role in our spiritual journey.

"And where the Spirit of the Lord is, there is freedom" offers a powerful promise. This freedom is not just a physical or external liberty but an internal, spiritual liberation. It encompasses freedom from the guilt and condemnation of sin, freedom from the burdens of legalism and self-reliance, and freedom to live in the fullness of God's grace. The Spirit brings about a transformation that allows us to live in a way that is aligned with God's will, characterized by joy, peace, and righteousness.

This verse invites us to embrace the freedom that comes through the Spirit. It encourages us to allow the Holy Spirit to guide and shape our lives, leading us away from the constraints of sin and legalism into a life of true freedom in Christ. This freedom empowers us to live boldly and authentically, knowing that we are accepted and loved by God.

Prayer

Heavenly Father,
Thank You for the promise in 2 Corinthians 3:17 that where
Your Spirit is, there is freedom. I am grateful for the freedom
You provide through the Holy Spirit, freeing me from sin and
legalism. Help me to live in this freedom daily, allowing the
Spirit to guide and transform my life. Teach me to embrace the
liberation You offer and to share this message of hope with
others.
In Jesus' name, Amen.

CONTEMPLATION

Spend a few moments in quiet reflection, inviting the
Holy Spirit to reveal areas where you need His
freedom. Allow His presence to bring liberation and
peace, and open your heart to His transformative work.

DAY 56
Experiencing the Depth of God's Love

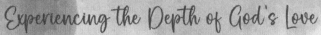

1 John 4:16 (NIV)

"So we have come to know and to believe the love that God has for us. God is love. Whoever abides in love abides in God, and God abides in them."

Devotional

1 John 4:16 encapsulates the core of Christian faith by emphasizing the profound and transformative nature of God's love. This verse reveals the depth of the relationship between God, His love, and those who dwell in Him.

"So we have come to know and to believe the love that God has for us" speaks to a deep, personal knowledge and belief in God's love. This love is not just a concept or an abstract idea but a tangible reality that believers experience and trust. It is through a personal relationship with God that we come to fully understand and embrace the extent of His love.

"God is love" is a defining statement about God's very nature. Unlike human love, which can be fickle and conditional, God's love is constant, unchanging, and unconditional. This divine love is the foundation of our relationship with Him and the basis of our identity as His children.

"Whoever abides in love abides in God, and God abides in them" highlights the reciprocal nature of our relationship with God. To "abide" means to remain or dwell in a state of continuous connection. When we choose to live in love, we align ourselves with God's nature, and He remains in us. This mutual indwelling leads to a transformed life where His love flows through us, impacting our relationships and actions.

This verse encourages us to cultivate an ongoing awareness of and commitment to God's love. It invites us to remain in that love and to let it shape who we are and how we interact with others.

Prayer

Heavenly Father,
I thank You for the incredible love You have for me, as described in 1 John 4:16. I am amazed by the depth of Your love and grateful for the relationship I have with You. Help me to abide in Your love, allowing it to shape my life and guide my actions. Teach me to reflect Your love to others and to remain in the security of Your constant presence.
In Jesus' name, Amen.

CONTEMPLATION

Spend a few moments in quiet reflection, allowing God's love to fill your heart. Let His love resonate deeply within you, and consider how you can actively live out and share this love in your daily life.

DAY 57
Trusting in God's Faithfulness

Psalm 9:10 (NIV)
"Those who know your name trust in you, for you, Lord, have never forsaken those who seek you."

Devotional

Psalm 9:10 is a powerful reminder of the trustworthiness and faithfulness of God. This verse emphasizes the deep connection between knowing God's character and having confidence in His promises.

"Those who know your name trust in you" points to the relationship between familiarity with God and trust in Him. Knowing God's name in the biblical sense means understanding His nature and character. His name represents His essence—His love, justice, mercy, and faithfulness. As we come to know these aspects of God through His Word and our experiences with Him, our trust in Him grows stronger. This trust is not based on fleeting feelings but on a profound understanding of who God is and what He has promised.

"For you, Lord, have never forsaken those who seek you" offers a reassuring promise. God's faithfulness is unwavering; He has never abandoned those who earnestly seek Him. This promise is a source of immense comfort and encouragement. It assures us that no matter the circumstances we face, God remains steadfast and present. He does not turn away from us in times of trouble but remains with us, guiding and supporting us through every challenge.

This verse invites us to deepen our knowledge of God, which in turn enhances our trust in Him. It encourages us to seek Him diligently, knowing that He will never forsake us. As we grow in our understanding of God's character, our trust in His provision and care becomes more secure.

Prayer

Heavenly Father,

I am grateful for Your promise in Psalm 9:10 that You never forsake those who seek You. I desire to know You more deeply and to trust in Your faithfulness. Help me to grow in my understanding of Your character and to seek You diligently. Strengthen my trust in Your promises, and let Your presence bring comfort and assurance in all circumstances.
In Jesus' name, Amen.

CONTEMPLATION

Spend a few moments in quiet reflection, focusing on the attributes of God revealed in Scripture. Allow this understanding to deepen your trust in Him, and rest in the assurance that He will never forsake you.

DAY 58
Finding Peace in God's Provision

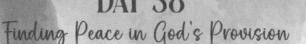

Psalm 68:6 (NIV)

"God sets the lonely in families, he leads out the prisoners with singing; but the rebellious live in a sun-scorched land."

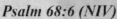

Devotional

Psalm 68:6 provides a vivid picture of God's compassionate care and provision for those in need. This verse contrasts the blessings of those who align with God's ways and the desolation that comes from rebellion.

"God sets the lonely in families" is a profound testament to God's heart for the isolated and brokenhearted. Loneliness and isolation can be deeply painful, but this verse promises that God provides a sense of belonging and community. By placing the lonely "in families," God extends His love and care through relationships and support systems, offering comfort and connection. This can be seen as both a literal placement into family units and a metaphorical inclusion into the larger family of faith.

"He leads out the prisoners with singing" illustrates God's power to bring freedom and joy. Prisoners here can be understood not just as those in physical captivity but also as those imprisoned by their circumstances or struggles. God's ability to lead them out with singing represents a transformative release from their burdens and a restoration of joy. This freedom is not merely physical but deeply spiritual and emotional, reflecting God's redemptive work in our lives.

"But the rebellious live in a sun-scorched land" serves as a caution. Rebellion against God's ways leads to a place of desolation and spiritual dryness. It contrasts starkly with the flourishing and provision experienced by those who follow God. This imagery underscores the consequences of living apart from God's guidance and grace.

Prayer

Heavenly Father,

I am grateful for the promise in Psalm 68:6 that You set the lonely in families and lead the prisoners out with singing. Thank You for Your provision and care in my life. Help me to embrace the community You have placed around me and to find freedom and joy in Your presence. Guide me away from rebellion and towards Your ways, that I might experience the fullness of Your blessings.

In Jesus' name, Amen.

CONTEMPLATION

Spend a few moments in quiet reflection, acknowledging the ways God has provided for you and brought you into a supportive community. Allow His peace and joy to fill your heart, and consider how you can further align with His will in your life.

DAY 59
Confidence in Prayer

1 John 5:14 (NIV)
"This is the confidence we have in approaching God: that if we ask anything according to his will, he hears us."

Devotional

1 John 5:14 is a powerful verse that speaks to the confidence and assurance we can have in our relationship with God, particularly when it comes to prayer. It highlights the foundational truth that our prayers are heard and answered when aligned with God's will.

"This is the confidence we have in approaching God" sets the tone for understanding how we can approach our Heavenly Father with boldness and assurance. Confidence in prayer is not based on our merit or eloquence but on our relationship with God and His promises. It invites us to approach God with the assurance that He is attentive and responsive to our petitions.

"That if we ask anything according to his will, he hears us" provides a key condition for effective prayer. The power of our prayers is linked to their alignment with God's will. This means that our requests should be in harmony with God's desires and purposes for our lives and the world. When we pray in accordance with His will, we can be confident that He not only hears but also acts in ways that are ultimately for our good and His glory.

This verse encourages us to seek a deeper understanding of God's will through prayer and Scripture. It invites us to trust in His wisdom and timing, knowing that our prayers are part of a larger divine plan.

Prayer

Heavenly Father,

Thank You for the assurance in 1 John 5:14 that we can approach You with confidence and that You hear our prayers when they are in accordance with Your will. Help me to align my requests with Your desires and to trust in Your perfect timing and wisdom. Teach me to pray with faith and confidence, knowing that You are always attentive to my needs. In Jesus' name, Amen.

CONTEMPLATION

Spend a few moments in quiet reflection, asking God to help you understand His will more deeply. Consider any specific prayers you have and how they align with His purposes. Rest in the confidence that God hears and responds to your prayers.

DAY 60
The Reward of Faith

Hebrews 11:6 (NIV)

"And without faith it is impossible to please God, because anyone who comes to him must believe that he exists and that he rewards those who earnestly seek him."

Devotional

Hebrews 11:6 is a cornerstone verse that highlights the essential role of faith in our relationship with God. It underscores the idea that faith is not merely a passive belief but an active, dynamic force that influences our entire approach to God and His promises.

"And without faith it is impossible to please God" emphasizes that faith is fundamental to our relationship with the Almighty. Faith is more than an intellectual assent; it is a trust and reliance on God that permeates every aspect of our lives. It is the starting point of our journey with God, and without it, our efforts to please Him fall short. Faith aligns our hearts with God's desires and opens the door to His transformative work in our lives.

"Because anyone who comes to him must believe that he exists" points to the necessity of recognizing and acknowledging God's existence. This foundational belief is crucial as it sets the stage for all further trust and relationship with Him. Belief in God's existence is the first step in a relationship that is marked by trust and dependence on His character and promises.

"And that he rewards those who earnestly seek him" offers a powerful promise. God is not only real but actively engaged in rewarding those who diligently seek Him. The reward here is not merely material but includes spiritual blessings such as peace, guidance, and a deeper relationship with God. Seeking Him earnestly means pursuing Him with a sincere and dedicated heart, trusting that He responds with generosity and grace.

Prayer

Heavenly Father,
I thank You for the promise in Hebrews 11:6 that faith is essential to pleasing You and that You reward those who earnestly seek You. Help me to grow in my faith, to truly believe in Your existence, and to seek You with a sincere heart. I trust in Your promises and seek Your guidance and blessings in my life.
In Jesus' name, Amen.

CONTEMPLATION

Spend a few moments in quiet reflection, asking God to deepen your faith and help you seek Him earnestly. Consider areas where you can grow in your trust and pursuit of God, and rest in the assurance of His rewards.

DAY 61
The Eternal Perspective

2 Corinthians 5:1 (NIV)
"For we know that if the earthly tent we live in is destroyed, we have a building from God, an eternal house in heaven, not built by human hands."

Devotional

2 Corinthians 5:1 offers a profound perspective on the transient nature of our earthly existence and the eternal security we have in Christ. The imagery of a "tent" versus a "building" highlights the contrast between our temporary, physical lives and our eternal, spiritual home.

"For we know that if the earthly tent we live in is destroyed" refers to our physical bodies, which are temporary and subject to decay. Paul uses the metaphor of a "tent" to emphasize the impermanence and fragility of our earthly existence. Just as a tent is a temporary shelter, our physical bodies are temporary vessels for our eternal selves.

"We have a building from God, an eternal house in heaven" shifts the focus to our eternal future. This "building" represents the secure, everlasting home prepared for us by God. Unlike the temporary tent, this eternal house is permanent and unshakable, reflecting the stability and permanence of our eternal life with God.

"Not built by human hands" underscores that this eternal home is divinely created, beyond the limitations and imperfections of human effort. It is a place crafted by God Himself, reflecting His perfect design and care for us. This assures us that our eternal home is secure and incomparable to anything we can create or imagine on earth.

This verse encourages us to adopt an eternal perspective, recognizing that while our earthly lives are temporary, we have the hope and promise of a permanent, glorious future with God. It calls us to live with the confidence that our ultimate security and hope are found in our relationship with Him.

Prayer

Heavenly Father,

Thank You for the promise of an eternal home with You as described in 2 Corinthians 5:1. I am grateful for the security and hope that comes from knowing that my earthly body is temporary but my eternal life is secure in Your hands. Help me to live with an eternal perspective, finding comfort and purpose in Your promises. May this assurance guide my actions and attitudes each day.

In Jesus' name, Amen.

CONTEMPLATION

Spend a few moments in quiet reflection, focusing on the contrast between your temporary earthly existence and your eternal future. Allow this perspective to fill you with peace and hope, and consider how it can influence your daily life.

DAY 62
The Promise of Victory

Revelation 3:21 (NIV)
"To the one who is victorious, I will give the right to sit with me on my throne, just as I was victorious and sat down with my Father on his throne."

Devotional
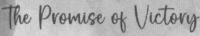

Isaiah 12:2 is a powerful declaration of faith and confidence in God as our ultimate source of salvation and strength.

The verse begins with a profound affirmation: "Surely God is my salvation." This statement acknowledges that God alone is the source of our ultimate deliverance. In a world filled with uncertainty and challenges, it is a comforting truth that our salvation is secure in God's hands. He is not just a part of our salvation but its entirety.

"I will trust and not be afraid" underscores the natural response to recognizing God as our salvation. Trust is a deliberate choice to rely on God's promises and character, while fear often comes from uncertainty and doubt. By placing our trust in God, we replace fear with faith, knowing that He is in control of every aspect of our lives.

"The Lord, the Lord himself, is my strength and my defense" highlights the dual role of God as both our source of power and our protector. In moments of weakness or vulnerability, we can lean on God's strength. In times of attack or danger, He is our defense. This double assurance of strength and protection provides a solid foundation for enduring life's trials.

"He has become my salvation" completes the verse with a note of personal relationship and fulfillment. God is not a distant or abstract concept but a personal savior who actively engages in our lives. This personal relationship transforms our understanding of salvation from a distant promise to an immediate and personal reality.

Prayer

Heavenly Father,

Thank You for the incredible promise in Revelation 3:21 that I will share in Christ's victory and sit with Him on His throne. Help me to remain faithful and steadfast, trusting in Your promises even amidst trials. Fill me with hope and assurance as I live out my faith, knowing that my perseverance will be rewarded. May this promise inspire me to encourage others in their journey of faith.

In Jesus' name, Amen.

CONTEMPLATION

Spend a few moments in quiet reflection, contemplating the promise of sharing in Christ's victory and eternal reign. Allow this promise to inspire and strengthen your faith, and consider how it can influence your daily life and interactions with others.

DAY 63
The Certainty of God's Promises

2 Corinthians 1:20 (NIV)
"For no matter how many promises God has made, they are 'Yes' in Christ. And so through him the 'Amen' is spoken by us to the glory of God."

Devotional

2 Corinthians 1:20 offers a profound reassurance about the nature of God's promises and their fulfillment through Jesus Christ. The verse highlights both the certainty and the scope of God's promises and invites us to respond with faith and affirmation.

'For no matter how many promises God has made' speaks to the vast and comprehensive nature of God's promises throughout Scripture. From the promises of provision, protection, and guidance to the promises of salvation and eternal life, God's assurances are numerous and varied. This verse reminds us that no matter how extensive or specific God's promises are, they all find their fulfillment in Christ.

'They are 'Yes' in Christ" underscores the certainty and affirmation of these promises. Jesus is the fulfillment and confirmation of God's promises. In Him, every promise of God is assured and brought to completion. This means that what God has pledged, He will deliver, because Christ is the guarantee and embodiment of God's faithfulness.

"And so through him the 'Amen' is spoken by us to the glory of God" reflects our response to this certainty. "Amen" means "so be it" or "let it be so," and when we say "Amen" through Christ, we affirm our trust in God's promises and acknowledge their fulfillment. This affirmation glorifies God, as it acknowledges His faithfulness and the truth of His Word.

This verse encourages us to rest in the confidence that every promise God has made is true and fulfilled in Christ. It calls us to respond with faith, trusting in God's reliability and giving glory to Him for His steadfastness.

Prayer

Heavenly Father,

I thank You for the assurance in 2 Corinthians 1:20 that all Your promises are "Yes" in Christ. I am grateful that Jesus is the fulfillment of every promise You have made. Help me to trust in Your promises with confidence and to respond with faith and affirmation. May my life reflect Your faithfulness and bring glory to You.

In Jesus' name, Amen.

CONTEMPLATION

Spend a few moments in quiet reflection, focusing on the promises of God and their fulfillment in Christ. Consider how this assurance can strengthen your faith and shape your responses to life's challenges.

DAY 64
Inscribed in God's Hand

Isaiah 49:16 (NIV)

"See, I have engraved you on the palms of my hands; your walls are ever before me."

Devotional

Isaiah 49:16 offers a beautiful picture of God's deep and unending care for His people. In this verse, God uses vivid imagery to convey His unwavering commitment and love.

"See, I have engraved you on the palms of my hands" illustrates a profound sense of intimacy and permanence. To be engraved means to be deeply and permanently marked. God is saying that each of His people is etched into His hands–a place of constant, unremovable presence. This image speaks to the depth of His commitment to us. Just as we might engrave something of great value to us, God has engraved us on His hands, signifying how precious and integral we are to Him.

"Your walls are ever before me" expands on this metaphor, suggesting that not only are we permanently marked by God, but He is continually attentive to our needs and struggles. The "walls" symbolize the protective and supportive aspects of our lives. God's gaze is ever upon us, ensuring our well-being and safeguarding us against adversity. His constant awareness assures us that He is always with us, attentive to our struggles and triumphs.

This verse reassures us of God's unceasing care and presence. Even when we feel overlooked or forgotten, we can be confident that we are always in His thoughts. His care for us is not fleeting but enduring, marked by a divine commitment that cannot be erased or diminished.

Prayer

Heavenly Father,

Thank You for the promise in Isaiah 49:16 that You have engraved me on the palms of Your hands. I am grateful for the depth of Your love and the assurance of Your constant presence. Help me to remember that I am always in Your thoughts and care. May this truth bring me comfort and strength, and may I share this assurance with others who need to know Your enduring love.

In Jesus' name, Amen.

CONTEMPLATION

Spend a few moments in quiet reflection, focusing on the image of being engraved on God's hands. Consider how this assurance impacts your view of yourself and your relationship with God. Let this truth encourage and strengthen you in your daily walk with Him.

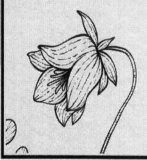

DAY 65
The Promise of Harvest

Galatians 6:9 (NIV)
"Let us not become weary in doing good, for at the proper time we will reap a harvest if we do not give up."

Devotional

Galatians 6:9 offers a powerful encouragement for those who are striving to live a life of faith and good works. The verse speaks directly to the heart of perseverance and the reward that comes from steadfastness in doing good.

"Let us not become weary in doing good" acknowledges the reality that doing good can sometimes be challenging and draining. Whether it's serving others, maintaining integrity, or pursuing justice, the path of righteousness often involves effort and sacrifice. The call here is to resist the temptation to grow tired or discouraged in the face of these challenges. It's a reminder that our efforts, even when they seem unnoticed or unrewarded, are significant in the eyes of God.

"For at the proper time we will reap a harvest" provides a hopeful promise. Just as a farmer plants seeds and waits patiently for them to grow, we too must trust that our diligent efforts will eventually yield results. The "harvest" represents the blessings and outcomes of our labor in faith—whether it be personal growth, the positive impact on others, or the fulfillment of God's plans in our lives. The key is to trust in God's timing and to remain faithful despite any current lack of visible results.

"If we do not give up" highlights the importance of persistence. The reward is assured, but it comes to those who endure. Giving up is not an option if we are to see the fruits of our labor. This encouragement calls us to remain steadfast and continue our good works with patience and faith, knowing that our efforts will be fruitful in due season.

Prayer

Heavenly Father,
Thank You for the encouragement found in Galatians 6:9. Help me to not grow weary in doing good, even when the results seem distant or unseen. Strengthen my faith and grant me patience to wait for the harvest You have promised. May I persevere in my efforts, trusting in Your perfect timing and the fruitfulness that will come.
In Jesus' name, Amen.

CONTEMPLATION

Spend a few moments in quiet reflection, focusing on areas where you may need renewed strength and perseverance. Ask God to help you maintain your commitment to doing good and to trust in His promises for the harvest.

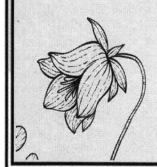

DAY 66
The Power of Humility

1 Peter 5:6 (NIV)
"Humble yourselves, therefore, under God's mighty hand, that he may lift you up in due time."

Devotional

1 Peter 5:6 offers profound wisdom about the posture we should adopt in our relationship with God. This verse highlights the importance of humility and the promise of God's exaltation in His perfect timing.

"Humble yourselves, therefore, under God's mighty hand" calls us to adopt a stance of humility before God. To humble oneself is to recognize our own limitations and the vastness of God's power and grace. This act of surrender involves acknowledging that we are not in control of our own lives, but that God's hand is both powerful and benevolent. By submitting to God's authority and trusting in His plans, we align ourselves with His will and open ourselves up to His guidance and provision.

"That he may lift you up in due time" assures us of God's promise to exalt those who remain humble. The phrase "in due time" is crucial here, as it points to the fact that God's timing is perfect, even if it doesn't align with our own expectations. This promise is not about immediate gratification but about the assurance that God will elevate us according to His divine plan and timing. His lifting up is not only about physical or material blessings but also about spiritual growth and fulfillment.

This verse encourages us to relinquish our own agendas and trust in God's timing and purposes. It is a call to trust that God's plans are better than our own and that His ways of lifting us up will be far greater and more meaningful than anything we could achieve on our own.

Prayer

Heavenly Father,
Thank You for the promise in 1 Peter 5:6 that if I humble myself under Your mighty hand, You will lift me up in due time. Help me to practice humility in all areas of my life and to trust in Your perfect timing. Teach me to surrender my plans to You and to wait patiently for Your elevation. May my life reflect Your grace and wisdom.
In Jesus' name, Amen.

CONTEMPLATION

Spend a few moments in quiet reflection, focusing on areas where you might need to humble yourself before God. Consider how you can trust in His timing and how this trust can impact your daily life and decisions.

DAY 67
The Call to Mercy

James 2:13 (NIV)
"Because judgment without mercy will be shown to anyone who has not been merciful. Mercy triumphs over judgment."

Devotional

James 2:13 is a poignant reminder of the crucial role mercy plays in our lives as Christians. This verse offers a clear directive about how we should interact with others and the profound impact of mercy in the life of a believer.

"Judgment without mercy will be shown to anyone who has not been merciful" warns us that our treatment of others is closely tied to how we will be treated. It emphasizes that a lack of mercy in our interactions can lead to a harsh and unyielding judgment. This doesn't mean that God's judgment is merely about our actions, but rather that our actions reflect the state of our hearts. If we withhold mercy, we risk experiencing a similar lack of mercy in return.

"Mercy triumphs over judgment" is a powerful declaration that mercy has the final say. It underscores that while judgment is a part of life, mercy holds the ultimate power to overcome it. Mercy here is not just a passive quality but an active force that brings about reconciliation, healing, and transformation. It speaks to the essence of God's grace and love—a reminder that, despite our failings, God's mercy prevails and provides us with forgiveness and grace.

This verse calls us to reflect on how we show mercy in our own lives. Are we quick to judge, or do we extend compassion and understanding? It challenges us to align our behavior with the merciful character of God, recognizing that mercy is not only a virtue but a divine mandate.

Prayer

Heavenly Father,

Thank You for the profound truth in James 2:13 that mercy triumphs over judgment. Help me to be a vessel of Your mercy in all my interactions. Forgive me for the times I have been quick to judge and slow to show compassion. Fill my heart with Your grace and teach me to extend mercy as You have done for me. May my actions reflect Your love and bring glory to Your name. In Jesus' name, Amen.

CONTEMPLATION

Spend a few moments in quiet reflection, considering areas where you might need to practice mercy.
Ask God to help you embody His mercy and to guide you in extending grace to others in your life.

DAY 68
The Power of the Spirit Within Us

Romans 8:11 (NIV)

"And if the Spirit of him who raised Jesus from the dead is living in you, he who raised Christ from the dead will also give life to your mortal bodies because of his Spirit who lives in you."

Devotional

Romans 8:11 offers a profound assurance of the transformative power available to us through the Holy Spirit. This verse speaks to the incredible reality that the same divine power that raised Jesus from the dead is at work within us.

"And if the Spirit of him who raised Jesus from the dead is living in you" emphasizes the connection between the Holy Spirit and the resurrection power. The Holy Spirit, who is the very essence of God's power, resides within every believer. This is not just a theoretical or distant concept but a present and personal reality. It means that the same Spirit who conquered death and brought Jesus back to life is actively present in our lives, empowering us beyond our natural abilities.

"He who raised Christ from the dead will also give life to your mortal bodies" assures us of the transformative impact of this divine presence. This isn't limited to physical resurrection but also includes new vitality, spiritual strength, and renewed hope. The Spirit's work extends to revitalizing our lives, giving us the power to overcome challenges, face trials, and live victoriously. It promises that our mortal bodies are not bound by the limitations of sin and decay but are enlivened by the Spirit's renewing power.

"Because of his Spirit who lives in you" highlights the personal nature of this promise. The indwelling Spirit is not just a force but a personal presence who guides, comforts, and strengthens us. This relationship with the Holy Spirit is the source of our spiritual renewal and empowerment.

Prayer

Heavenly Father,
Thank You for the incredible promise in Romans 8:11 that Your Spirit, who raised Jesus from the dead, lives within me. Help me to fully embrace the power and renewal that comes from Your Holy Spirit. Strengthen me in my weaknesses and empower me to live victoriously. May Your Spirit guide me and give me life in all areas of my life.
In Jesus' name, Amen.

CONTEMPLATION

Spend a few moments in quiet reflection, considering how the Holy Spirit's power is at work in your life. Reflect on areas where you need His strength and renewal and seek His presence in those areas.

DAY 69
Hidden with Christ

Colossians 3:3 (NIV)
"For you died, and your life is now hidden with Christ in God."

Devotional

Colossians 3:3 provides a profound insight into the identity and security we have as believers in Christ. This verse offers both comfort and challenge, reminding us of the transformative relationship we have with Jesus and the new life we possess.

"For you died" speaks to the reality of our spiritual transformation. In Christ, our old self—the person we were before coming to faith—has died. This death signifies the end of our former way of life, characterized by sin and separation from God. By dying with Christ, we have been released from the power of sin and its hold on us. This is not merely a symbolic act but a profound spiritual reality that changes the very essence of who we are.

"Your life is now hidden with Christ in God" presents a powerful image of security and intimacy. Our new life in Christ is "hidden" with Him, meaning that our true identity and essence are now safely secured in Him. This hiddenness signifies a place of protection and sanctity—our life is safeguarded in the presence of God. To be "hidden" with Christ implies that our worth and value are found in Him, and nothing can separate us from this secure position. It also suggests that our future and our true selves are bound up with Christ, beyond the reach of earthly trials and uncertainties.

This verse encourages us to live in light of this new reality. Knowing that our life is hidden with Christ should impact how we face challenges and make decisions. We can approach life with confidence, knowing that our identity is secure and that our ultimate hope is anchored in Christ.

Prayer

Heavenly Father,
Thank You for the truth found in Colossians 3:3–that my life is hidden with Christ in You. Help me to fully embrace my new identity in Christ and to live with the confidence and security that comes from being united with Him. May this truth guide my decisions and bring me peace, knowing that my worth and future are securely anchored in You.
In Jesus' name, Amen.

CONTEMPLATION

Spend a few moments in quiet reflection, focusing on the reality that your life is hidden with Christ in God. Reflect on how this truth can impact your daily life and seek God's guidance in living out your new identity.

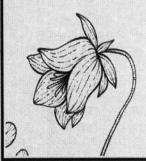

DAY 70
Drawing Near to God

Ephesians 2:13 (NIV)

"But now in Christ Jesus you who once were far away have been brought near by the blood of Christ."

Devotional

Ephesians 2:13 highlights one of the most profound aspects of our relationship with God through Jesus Christ: the transition from being distant to being brought near. This verse is a powerful reminder of the reconciliation and closeness we now enjoy with God.

"But now in Christ Jesus" marks a significant turning point in our spiritual journey. It contrasts our former state with our current reality. Before Christ, we were separated from God, estranged by our sins and alienation. This distance was not just a physical one but a spiritual chasm, separating us from the life and relationship God intended for us.

"You who once were far away have been brought near by the blood of Christ" describes the transformative work of Jesus' sacrifice. The "blood of Christ" symbolizes the ultimate price Jesus paid to bridge the gap between humanity and God. His sacrifice on the cross removed the barrier of sin that kept us at a distance. Through His blood, we are not only forgiven but also granted intimate access to God. This nearness signifies a restored relationship where we can experience God's love, grace, and guidance directly.

This verse encourages us to fully embrace and appreciate the nearness we have with God. It invites us to live in the reality of this close relationship, accessing the comfort and strength that comes from being in His presence. Understanding that we are brought near by Christ's sacrifice should inspire us to approach God with confidence and gratitude, knowing that we have been reconciled and welcomed into His family.

Prayer

Heavenly Father,
Thank You for the incredible gift of nearness through Jesus
Christ. I am grateful for the reconciliation and intimacy that
Your blood has provided. Help me to live in the reality of this
closeness, approaching You with confidence and gratitude. May
my life reflect the joy and peace of being brought near to You,
and may I share this good news with others.
In Jesus' name, Amen.

CONTEMPLATION

Spend a few moments in quiet reflection, thanking God
for the nearness you have with Him through Jesus
Christ. Consider how this closeness impacts your life
and how you can live out the reality of this relationship
in practical ways.

DAY 71
Embracing the Father's Revelation

Matthew 11:25-26 (NIV)

"At that time Jesus said, 'I praise you, Father, Lord of heaven and earth, because you have hidden these things from the wise and learned, and revealed them to little children. Yes, Father, for this is what you were pleased to do.'"

Devotional

In Matthew 11:25-26, Jesus expresses profound gratitude to God for His ways of revealing truth. This passage offers a deep insight into how God's revelation operates and how we can embrace it in our lives.

Jesus begins with praise, acknowledging God as the "Lord of heaven and earth," which underscores His supreme authority and the vast scope of His creation. This acknowledgment sets the stage for understanding that God's ways are far beyond human comprehension. The phrase "hidden these things from the wise and learned" reveals that divine truth is not always accessible through human wisdom alone. The "wise and learned" refers to those who rely solely on their intellect and self-sufficiency, often missing the deeper, spiritual truths of God's kingdom.

In contrast, Jesus praises God for revealing these truths to "little children." This is not a dismissal of intellectual pursuits but an affirmation that understanding God's ways requires a childlike openness and humility. Children, in their simplicity and trust, are more receptive to the divine revelation that God offers. They approach with wonder and faith rather than relying on their own understanding.

"Yes, Father, for this is what you were pleased to do" signifies that God delights in this approach. It is God's pleasure to reveal Himself to those who come with humility and childlike faith. This revelation is not about intellectual achievement but about a heart that is open to receiving and embracing the truth of God's kingdom.

Prayer

Heavenly Father,
I thank You for the way You reveal Your truths to those who
come to You with childlike faith. Help me to approach You with
humility, trusting in Your wisdom and understanding. Open my
heart to receive the revelations You have for me and guide me in
living out Your truths. May I reflect the joy and simplicity of a
child in my relationship with You.
In Jesus' name, Amen.

CONTEMPLATION

Spend a few moments in quiet reflection, considering
how you approach God's truth. Ask Him to help you
adopt a childlike faith and openness, and listen for His
guidance in your heart.

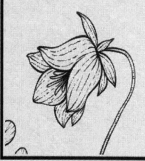

DAY 72
God's Choice in Our Weakness

1 Corinthians 1:27 (NIV)
"But God chose the foolish things of the world to shame the wise; God chose the weak things of the world to shame the strong."

Devotional

1 Corinthians 1:27 presents a profound truth about God's ways and His choices. This verse challenges worldly expectations and emphasizes a fundamental aspect of God's kingdom: He often works through what the world considers weak and foolish.

"But God chose the foolish things of the world to shame the wise" underscores God's pattern of using what seems insignificant or irrational by human standards to confound human wisdom. This divine choice reveals that God's perspective is far beyond our limited understanding. Where the world sees foolishness, God sees potential for His glory. This truth encourages us to value and embrace what the world might overlook or dismiss.

Similarly, "God chose the weak things of the world to shame the strong" highlights how God uses weakness to demonstrate His power. In a culture that idolizes strength and self-sufficiency, God's choice to use the weak shows that His strength is made perfect in our weakness (2 Corinthians 12:9). This not only defies conventional expectations but also shifts our focus from relying on our own strength to depending on God's power.

For us, this means that our perceived inadequacies or limitations are not barriers to God's use of us. Rather, they become the very canvas upon which His strength and wisdom are displayed. It reassures us that we don't need to be extraordinary in our own right to be used by God. Instead, our openness and availability to Him are what matter.

Prayer

Heavenly Father,
Thank You for choosing the foolish and weak things of the
world to display Your wisdom and strength. Help me to
embrace my own weaknesses and limitations, knowing that
Your power is perfected in them. Teach me to trust in Your ways
and to make myself available for Your work, regardless of how I
might perceive my own abilities. May my life reflect Your glory
and grace.
In Jesus' name, Amen.

CONTEMPLATION

Spend a few moments in quiet reflection, considering
how God might be calling you to embrace your
weaknesses and trust in His power. Seek His guidance
on how you can be available for His work, no matter
your own perceived limitations.

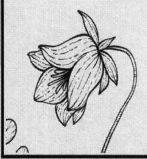

DAY 73
A Chosen People

1 Peter 2:9 (NIV)

"But you are a chosen people, a royal priesthood, a holy nation, God's special possession, that you may declare the praises of him who called you out of darkness into his wonderful light."

Devotional

1 Peter 2:9 is a powerful declaration of our identity and purpose in Christ. This verse highlights four profound truths about who we are as believers and the purpose to which we are called.

Firstly, "you are a chosen people" speaks to the incredible privilege of being selected by God. In a world where people often feel overlooked or unworthy, this verse reassures us that God has deliberately chosen us to be part of His family. This choice is not based on our merit but on His grace and love.

Secondly, we are described as "a royal priesthood." This imagery connects us to the roles of priests in the Old Testament who were intermediaries between God and His people. In Christ, we are invited into this role, not only to approach God directly but also to mediate His love and truth to others. Our lives are meant to reflect the holiness and compassion of God in our interactions with the world.

Thirdly, "a holy nation" emphasizes our identity as part of a distinct and sacred community. We are set apart by God, called to live according to His standards and to represent His values in a world that often contrasts with His ways. This holiness is not about isolation but about embodying God's character and purpose.

Finally, we are "God's special possession." This phrase captures the depth of God's commitment and love for us. We are treasured and valued by Him, and this identity forms the foundation of our self-worth and purpose.

Prayer

Heavenly Father,

Thank You for choosing me, for making me part of Your royal priesthood and holy nation. Help me to live out this identity with purpose and grace. May my life reflect Your light and declare Your praises. Enable me to embrace my role in Your kingdom and to share the incredible transformation You've brought into my life.

In Jesus' name, Amen.

CONTEMPLATION

Spend a few moments in quiet reflection, thanking God for your identity in Christ. Reflect on how you can live out these truths and share the light of His presence with others.

DAY 74
Peace in the Midst of Adversity

Psalm 91:7 (NIV)
"A thousand may fall at your side, ten thousand at your right hand, but it will not come near you."

Devotional

Psalm 91:7 offers profound reassurance in times of trouble. The imagery of a thousand falling at one side and ten thousand at the right hand paints a vivid picture of overwhelming adversity and chaos. Yet, this verse promises a remarkable truth: "but it will not come near you."

In the context of Psalm 91, this verse underscores God's protection over those who trust in Him. It highlights the reality that, despite the multitude of challenges or dangers that may surround us, God's steadfast presence and care create a shield around His people.

The promise here is not that we will be exempt from difficulties or threats, but that God's protection will preserve us through them. Even when it seems like everything around us is falling apart, God's faithfulness ensures that these trials will not ultimately harm us. His protection is not just a physical safeguard but a spiritual assurance that He is with us, providing peace and stability.

This verse encourages us to remain steadfast in our faith, trusting in God's ability to keep us safe amidst the storm. It invites us to look beyond immediate circumstances and focus on the eternal security we have in God. His protection allows us to face each day with courage and peace, knowing that He is sovereign and capable of guarding us against any harm.

Prayer

Heavenly Father,
Thank You for the promise of Your protection, even in the midst
of overwhelming trials. Help me to trust in Your faithfulness
and to find peace in Your presence. When I face adversity,
remind me that You are my refuge and shield. Strengthen my
faith and give me courage to stand firm, knowing that no matter
what happens, Your protection surrounds me.
In Jesus' name, Amen.

CONTEMPLATION

Spend a few moments in quiet reflection, focusing on
the areas where you need God's protection. Meditate on
His promise to shield you from harm and ask Him to
grant you peace and assurance in His care.

DAY 75
Strength for the Journey

2 Samuel 22:33-34 (NIV)

"It is God who arms me with strength and keeps my way secure. He makes my feet like the feet of a deer; he causes me to stand on the heights."

Devotional

In 2 Samuel 22:33-34, King David reflects on the profound truth of God's provision and strength in his life. These verses offer a powerful testimony of how God equips us to face life's challenges and empowers us to rise above our circumstances.

David begins by acknowledging that it is "God who arms me with strength." This statement emphasizes that our strength and abilities are not derived from ourselves but from God. In times of difficulty, it can be easy to rely on our own resources and understanding. However, David reminds us that true strength comes from God alone. He is our ultimate source of power and support.

The verse continues, "He keeps my way secure." This assurance speaks to God's faithfulness in guiding and protecting us. In a world full of uncertainties and dangers, it is comforting to know that God is steadfast in securing our paths and leading us safely through life's journey.

The imagery of "feet like the feet of a deer" and being "caused to stand on the heights" conveys a sense of agility, stability, and elevation. Deer are known for their sure-footedness and ability to navigate challenging terrain with ease. This metaphor illustrates how God grants us the ability to overcome obstacles and rise above difficulties. His strength enables us to stand firm and move forward with confidence, even in the face of trials.

Prayer

Heavenly Father,
I thank You for being my source of strength and security. Help me to rely on Your power and guidance in every situation. Grant me the agility and stability I need to overcome obstacles and rise above difficulties. I trust in Your provision and protection, knowing that You are with me every step of the way.
In Jesus' name, Amen.

CONTEMPLATION

Spend a few moments in quiet reflection, focusing on areas where you need God's strength and guidance. Meditate on His promise to provide stability and empower you for the journey ahead.

DAY 76
Wonderfully Made

Psalm 139:13 (NIV)
"For you created my inmost being; you knit me together in my mother's womb."

Devotional

Psalm 139:13 offers a profound reminder of God's intimate and purposeful creation of each one of us. This verse celebrates the meticulous care and intentionality with which God designed every aspect of our being.

The imagery of God "creating my inmost being" and "knitting me together" speaks to the intricate and personal nature of our creation. Unlike a mere assembly of parts, the process of knitting involves detailed craftsmanship and individual attention. Similarly, God's creation of us was not a hasty or random act but a deliberate and loving design. Each part of who we are—our physical attributes, our personality traits, and our inherent talents—was carefully crafted by our Creator.

Understanding that God has personally designed us can transform how we view ourselves. In a world that often emphasizes comparison and inadequacy, Psalm 139:13 reassures us that we are wonderfully made. We are not accidents or mere products of chance but the result of divine artistry. This truth can bring immense comfort and confidence, knowing that we are valued and significant in God's eyes.

This verse also challenges us to embrace our identity with gratitude and purpose. Recognizing that God has a specific design and purpose for each of us invites us to live in a way that honors our Creator. It encourages us to appreciate our unique qualities and to use them for His glory.

Prayer

Heavenly Father,

I am in awe of Your handiwork in creating me. Thank You for knitting me together with such care and purpose. Help me to embrace my identity with gratitude and to live in a way that honors Your design. Teach me to see myself through Your eyes and to use my unique gifts for Your glory.

In Jesus' name, Amen.

CONTEMPLATION

Spend a few moments in quiet reflection, thanking God for your unique design. Meditate on how His craftsmanship in your life can be a source of comfort and inspiration. Ask Him to help you fully embrace your identity and purpose in Him.

DAY 77
The Lord's Faithful Provision

Psalm 37:18 (NIV)
"The blameless spend their days under the Lord's care, and their inheritance will endure forever."

Devotional

Psalm 37:18 offers a comforting promise about the security and care that the Lord provides for those who live with integrity and trust in Him. This verse reassures us that God's faithfulness extends to all aspects of our lives, particularly when we align ourselves with His ways.

The phrase "the blameless spend their days under the Lord's care" highlights the protective and nurturing nature of God's relationship with those who seek to live righteously. The term "blameless" refers to those who are committed to walking in faith and obedience, not in perfection but in sincere devotion. In this context, "under the Lord's care" signifies a life enveloped in God's constant guidance, provision, and protection. It's a reminder that when we strive to live according to God's principles, we are enveloped in His loving care.

The second part of the verse, "their inheritance will endure forever," points to the eternal rewards and promises that God has prepared for those who are faithful. Unlike earthly possessions that are fleeting and subject to decay, the inheritance given by God is everlasting. This eternal inheritance includes spiritual blessings and the promise of a secure place in His kingdom, which will not fade away.

In times of uncertainty or challenge, Psalm 37:18 encourages us to maintain our faith and integrity, trusting that God's care will sustain us. It invites us to focus on the eternal perspective rather than being overwhelmed by temporary difficulties. Our actions rooted in faith and righteousness have lasting significance, anchored in God's enduring promises.

Prayer

Heavenly Father,

Thank You for Your unwavering care and the eternal inheritance You promise to those who trust in You. Help me to live with integrity and faith, knowing that my life is under Your watchful eye. Strengthen my trust in Your provision and keep my focus on the eternal rewards You have prepared. May Your care and promises bring peace and assurance to my heart. In Jesus' name, Amen.

CONTEMPLATION

Spend a few moments in quiet reflection, considering how God's care has been evident in your life. Meditate on the eternal inheritance you have in Him and how this promise can influence your daily walk of faith.

DAY 78
Empowered by the Breath of Life

Job 33:4 (NIV)
"The Spirit of God has made me; the breath of the Almighty gives me life."

Devotional

Job 33:4 is a profound reminder of the divine source of our existence and vitality. In this verse, Elihu speaks to Job, declaring that our creation and life come from the Spirit of God and the breath of the Almighty. This declaration underscores a fundamental truth about our relationship with God: He is the ultimate source of our being and the sustainer of our lives.

"The Spirit of God has made me" acknowledges that our very existence is a result of God's creative power. From the moment of our conception to every breath we take, God's Spirit is actively involved in sustaining and guiding us. This divine involvement extends beyond mere creation; it encompasses every aspect of our lives, shaping our character, purpose, and experiences.

"The breath of the Almighty gives me life" further emphasizes that life itself is a gift from God. Just as God breathed life into Adam in the Genesis account, He continues to give us life each day. This breath signifies not just physical life but also spiritual vitality and renewal. It is a reminder that our every breath is a testament to God's sustaining power and His intimate involvement in our lives.

Understanding this verse can profoundly affect how we view our daily existence and challenges. Knowing that our lives are continually upheld by God's breath encourages us to trust in His provision and embrace our purpose with confidence. It also calls us to honor God with our lives, recognizing that our very being is a gift and a reflection of His grace.

Prayer

Heavenly Father,

Thank You for the gift of life and the breath that sustains me each day. I am in awe of Your creative power and Your continual presence in my life. Help me to live with gratitude, embracing my purpose and honoring You in all that I do. May my life reflect Your grace and the divine breath You have given me.

In Jesus' name, Amen.

CONTEMPLATION

Take a moment to quietly reflect on the breath you take and the life you have. Meditate on the fact that each breath is a gift from God and a testament to His sustaining power. Let this awareness deepen your appreciation for His role in your life.

DAY 79
Anchored in Hope

Hebrews 6:17-18 (NIV)

"Because God wanted to make the unchanging nature of His purpose very clear to the heirs of what was promised, He confirmed it with an oath. God did this so that, by two unchangeable things in which it is impossible for God to lie, we who have fled to take hold of the hope set before us may be greatly encouraged."

Devotional

Hebrews 6:17-18 provides a powerful assurance of God's unwavering promises and the hope we have in Him. These verses remind us of the certainty and encouragement that come from trusting in God's promises.

In these verses, the author highlights two crucial elements that underscore God's reliability: His unchanging nature and His oath. The "unchanging nature of His purpose" speaks to the constancy of God's plans and promises. Unlike human plans that can falter or change, God's purposes are steadfast and secure.

To further reinforce the certainty of His promises, God has "confirmed it with an oath." This divine oath serves as a double assurance, making it clear that God's promises are immutable and trustworthy. When God makes a promise and backs it with an oath, it is an unbreakable guarantee. This is a significant comfort, knowing that God's word is reliable and that He will fulfill His promises.

The result of this divine assurance is the hope that is set before us. "We who have fled to take hold of the hope set before us" signifies that, as believers, we find refuge and encouragement in God's promises. This hope is not a vague or uncertain wish but a firm and secure anchor for our souls. It is a hope that remains steadfast despite the trials and uncertainties of life.

Prayer

Heavenly Father,
I thank You for the unchanging nature of Your purpose and the assurance of Your promises. I am grateful for the hope that You provide, which serves as an anchor for my soul. Help me to trust in Your promises and find encouragement in Your steadfast love. May this hope strengthen me and inspire me to share Your assurance with others.
In Jesus' name, Amen.

CONTEMPLATION

Spend a few moments in quiet reflection, considering the promises of God and how they have been fulfilled in your life. Meditate on the hope that anchors you and allows it to bring peace and assurance to your heart.

DAY 80
The Joyful Return

Isaiah 51:11 (NIV)

*"Those the Lord has rescued will return. They will enter Zion with singing;
everlasting joy will crown their heads. Gladness and joy will overtake them, and
sorrow and sighing will flee away."*

Devotional

Isaiah 51:11 is a beautiful promise of restoration and joy for those who have
been rescued by the Lord. This verse speaks of a time when God's people,
once rescued from distress, will return to a place of peace and joy. It's a
powerful reminder of the transformative and redemptive nature of God's
intervention in our lives.

The verse begins with the assurance that "those the Lord has rescued will
return." This promise is rooted in the reality that God's deliverance leads
to restoration. The concept of returning here signifies not just a physical
return but a return to a state of spiritual and emotional well-being. It's an
invitation to trust in God's ability to bring us back from difficult and
sorrowful places to a place of joy and peace.

"They will enter Zion with singing" describes the joyful and triumphant
entry into a place of blessing and fulfillment. Zion represents not only a
physical location but also a symbol of God's promises and blessings.
Entering with singing denotes a heart filled with gratitude and celebration
for the deliverance experienced.

The promise of "everlasting joy" and the image of joy crowning their heads
suggest that the joy provided by God is profound and enduring. It's a joy
that goes beyond temporary circumstances and endures through all of
life's trials. This joy is so overwhelming that "gladness and joy will
overtake them," while "sorrow and sighing will flee away." It's an assurance
that God's intervention brings about a complete and total transformation,
where past sorrows are replaced with enduring joy.

Prayer

Heavenly Father,

I am grateful for the promise of Your deliverance and the everlasting joy You provide. Thank You for rescuing me and for the transformation You bring into my life. Help me to embrace the joy You offer and to let it replace any sorrow or sighing. Strengthen my faith in Your ability to restore and renew, and help me to share this hope with others.

In Jesus' name, Amen.

CONTEMPLATION

Spend a few moments in quiet reflection, meditating on the joy and restoration that God has promised. Consider how His deliverance has impacted your life and let this promise bring peace and hope to your heart.

DAY 81
The Promise of a New Beginning

Revelation 21:4 (NIV)
"He will wipe every tear from their eyes. There will be no more death or mourning or crying or pain, for the old order of things has passed away.'"

Devotional

Revelation 21:4 is a deeply comforting and hopeful promise that speaks to the ultimate restoration and renewal God has planned for us. In this verse, we find a glimpse of the future that awaits us in God's perfect kingdom—a future where sorrow, suffering, and pain are completely eradicated.

The verse begins with the tender promise, "He will wipe every tear from their eyes." This imagery of God personally wiping away our tears is profoundly intimate and reassuring. It portrays a God who is not distant but deeply involved in our healing and comfort. The act of wiping away tears symbolizes a complete and compassionate removal of our grief and suffering.

The promise that "there will be no more death or mourning or crying or pain" offers a vision of life in its purest form—free from the struggles and trials that characterize our current existence. Death, mourning, crying, and pain are all part of the fallen world we live in, but God assures us that these will be no more in His eternal kingdom. The phrase "the old order of things has passed away" signifies that God is making everything new, transforming our current reality into one of perfect peace and joy.

This promise invites us to look beyond our present difficulties and find hope in the future God has prepared. It assures us that our current suffering is temporary and that God's ultimate plan involves a complete restoration of all things.

Prayer

Heavenly Father,

Thank You for the promise of a future free from tears, pain, and suffering. I am grateful for Your assurance that You will wipe away every tear and make all things new. Help me to find comfort and hope in this promise, and to live with the confidence that my present troubles are temporary. Strengthen my faith and use me to encourage others with the hope of Your eternal kingdom.

In Jesus' name, Amen.

CONTEMPLATION

Take a few moments to meditate on the future promise described in this verse. Reflect on the comfort it brings and allow it to fill you with hope and peace, knowing that God's ultimate plan is for a world without suffering.

DAY 82
Draw Near to God

James 4:8 (NIV)
"Come near to God and he will come near to you. Wash your hands, you sinners, and purify your hearts, you double-minded."

Devotional

James 4:8 offers a powerful invitation and promise that beckons us into a deeper relationship with God. It underscores the transformative potential of drawing near to God and the reciprocal nature of this divine intimacy.

The verse begins with a clear call: "Come near to God." This invitation is both a challenge and a comfort. It challenges us to seek God with intentionality, to approach Him with our whole hearts and earnest desires. Coming near to God involves more than physical proximity; it requires a sincere and deliberate effort to deepen our spiritual connection with Him.

The promise that follows is profoundly reassuring: "He will come near to you." This is a divine assurance that when we make the move toward God, He responds with His presence. The idea that God will draw near to us emphasizes His willingness to be close and involved in our lives, meeting us where we are and guiding us into greater intimacy with Him.

James then calls us to a life of purity: "Wash your hands, you sinners, and purify your hearts, you double-minded." This call to cleanse ourselves signifies a movement towards spiritual and moral purity. It's an encouragement to remove sin from our lives and align our hearts fully with God's will. The act of washing hands and purifying hearts symbolizes the repentance and transformation necessary for a genuine relationship with God. It invites us to leave behind the duplicity and embrace a singular devotion to Him.

Prayer

Heavenly Father,
I am grateful for Your promise to draw near when I seek You.
Help me to approach You with sincerity and to purify my heart
from anything that hinders our relationship. I desire to be close
to You and to experience the fullness of Your presence in my life.
Guide me in this journey of transformation and help me to
encourage others to draw near to You as well.
In Jesus' name, Amen.

CONTEMPLATION

Spend a few moments in quiet reflection, considering
how you can draw nearer to God today. Meditate on the
ways He has been present in your life and let His
promise of nearness fill you with peace and
encouragement.

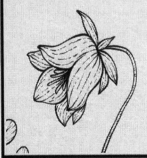

DAY 83
The Beloved Resting Place

Deuteronomy 33:12 (NIV)

"About Benjamin he said: 'Let the beloved of the Lord rest secure in him, for he shields him all day long, and the one the Lord loves rests between his shoulders.'"

Devotional

Deuteronomy 33:12 offers a profound expression of God's protective and loving care. This verse, spoken by Moses as he blesses the tribes of Israel, highlights the special relationship between God and His people, using Benjamin as a symbol of divine favor and security.

"Let the beloved of the Lord rest secure in him." This part of the verse assures us of God's unwavering love and the security that comes from resting in His presence. To be "beloved of the Lord" signifies being cherished and valued by God, a central truth for every believer. This promise invites us to find our peace and assurance in God, knowing that His love provides a steadfast foundation.

"For he shields him all day long" speaks to the comprehensive nature of God's protection. It's not just occasional or partial; it's constant and encompassing. God's shield is ever-present, guarding us from harm and guiding us through each day's challenges. This divine protection assures us that we are safe within His care, no matter the circumstances we face.

"The one the Lord loves rests between his shoulders" paints a picture of intimate care and closeness. In ancient times, carrying someone on one's shoulders was a gesture of trust and endearment. This imagery evokes the sense of being held securely by God, as if resting on His shoulders, close to His heart. It's a metaphor for the comfort and security that come from being fully embraced by God's love.

Prayer

Heavenly Father,
I am deeply grateful for Your love and protection. Thank You for being a shield that guards me all day long and for the comfort of resting in Your embrace. Help me to trust fully in Your care and to find peace in Your presence. May I share this assurance with others and reflect Your love in all I do.
In Jesus' name, Amen.

CONTEMPLATION

Spend a few moments in quiet reflection, imagining yourself resting securely in God's care. Consider how His love and protection have been evident in your life and let this promise bring peace and assurance to your heart.

DAY 84
Our Salvation Song

Isaiah 12:2 (NIV)
"Surely God is my salvation; I will trust and not be afraid. The Lord, the Lord himself, is my strength and my defense; he has become my salvation."

Devotional

Isaiah 12:2 is a powerful declaration of faith and confidence in God as our ultimate source of salvation and strength.

The verse begins with a profound affirmation: "Surely God is my salvation." This statement acknowledges that God alone is the source of our ultimate deliverance. In a world filled with uncertainty and challenges, it is a comforting truth that our salvation is secure in God's hands. He is not just a part of our salvation but its entirety.

"I will trust and not be afraid" underscores the natural response to recognizing God as our salvation. Trust is a deliberate choice to rely on God's promises and character, while fear often comes from uncertainty and doubt. By placing our trust in God, we replace fear with faith, knowing that He is in control of every aspect of our lives.

"The Lord, the Lord himself, is my strength and my defense" highlights the dual role of God as both our source of power and our protector. In moments of weakness or vulnerability, we can lean on God's strength. In times of attack or danger, He is our defense. This double assurance of strength and protection provides a solid foundation for enduring life's trials.

"He has become my salvation" completes the verse with a note of personal relationship and fulfillment. God is not a distant or abstract concept but a personal savior who actively engages in our lives. This personal relationship transforms our understanding of salvation from a distant promise to an immediate and personal reality.

Prayer

Heavenly Father,

I thank You for being my salvation, strength, and defense. Help me to trust in You fully and to overcome fear with the confidence that You are in control. May Your presence be my source of strength and protection in every situation. I am grateful for the personal relationship we share and for Your active role in my life.

In Jesus' name, Amen.

CONTEMPLATION

Spend a few moments in quiet reflection, focusing on God as your salvation and source of strength. Consider how His presence has been evident in your life and let this assurance fill you with peace and confidence.

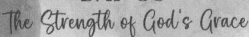

DAY 85
The Strength of God's Grace

2 Samuel 22:36 (NIV)

"You give me your shield of victory; you stoop down to make me great."

Devotional

2 Samuel 22:36 is a verse that beautifully captures the dual nature of God's interaction with us—His provision of protection and His elevation of our status. Spoken by David in his song of thanksgiving, this verse acknowledges God's role as both a shield and a source of greatness.

"You give me your shield of victory" speaks to the protection and defense that God provides. In biblical times, a shield was a crucial piece of armor used to defend against attacks. By describing God's protection as a "shield of victory," David is emphasizing that God's defense ensures not just survival but triumph over adversities. This imagery assures us that God's protection is not only about keeping us safe but also about leading us to victory in our struggles.

"You stoop down to make me great" reveals a tender aspect of God's character. The notion of God "stooping down" conveys His humility and willingness to engage with us on a personal level. Despite His majesty and power, God reaches down to elevate us, lifting us from our lowly state to a place of honor and significance. This act of grace highlights the incredible truth that God is not distant or aloof but actively involved in our lives, promoting our growth and success.

This verse invites us to reflect on the ways God's grace and protection have played out in our own lives. It encourages us to recognize that God's involvement is not limited to distant or grand acts but includes personal, intimate actions that lift us up and shield us from harm.

Prayer

Heavenly Father,
I thank You for being my shield of victory and for stooping down to make me great. Your protection and grace are beyond measure, and I am grateful for Your involvement in my life. Help me to recognize Your hand in my victories and to embrace the greatness You've provided through Your grace. May I live with a heart full of gratitude and extend Your love and encouragement to others.
In Jesus' name, Amen.

CONTEMPLATION

Spend a few moments in quiet reflection, focusing on the ways God has protected and elevated you. Consider how His grace has been evident in your life and let this assurance inspire a deep sense of peace and gratitude.

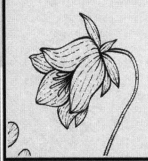

DAY 86
Wisdom Generously Given

James 1:5 (NIV)
"If any of you lacks wisdom, you should ask God, who gives generously to all without finding fault, and it will be given to you."

Devotional

James 1:5 is a profound invitation to seek divine wisdom and a promise of God's generous provision. This verse reassures us that in times of uncertainty or decision-making, we are not left to rely solely on our own understanding. Instead, we have the opportunity to access God's boundless wisdom.

"If any of you lacks wisdom" recognizes our human limitations. We all face moments when we feel uncertain or in need of guidance, whether in personal decisions, relationships, or understanding God's will. This acknowledgment is the starting point for seeking divine help, a humble admission that we cannot navigate life's complexities on our own.

"You should ask God, who gives generously to all without finding fault" highlights the nature of God's generosity. Unlike human interactions, where we might be judged or find fault, God's giving is characterized by grace and openness. He is always willing to impart wisdom freely to those who seek it, regardless of their past mistakes or current shortcomings. This generous and non-judgmental nature of God ensures that we can approach Him with confidence and expectation.

"And it will be given to you" is a powerful promise. It assures us that when we earnestly seek wisdom from God, He will provide it. This is not a conditional or limited promise but a guaranteed outcome. God's commitment to granting wisdom underscores His desire for us to live wisely and make decisions aligned with His will.

Prayer

Heavenly Father,
I come to You acknowledging my need for wisdom. Thank You
for Your promise to give generously and without judgment.
Please grant me the wisdom I need for the decisions and
challenges I face. Help me to trust in Your guidance and to act
upon the wisdom You provide. May Your wisdom shine through
in my life and be a blessing to others.
In Jesus' name, Amen.

CONTEMPLATION

Spend a few moments in quiet reflection, focusing on
areas where you need God's wisdom. Invite Him to
speak into those areas and listen for His guidance. Let
this assurance of His generous provision fill you with
peace and clarity.

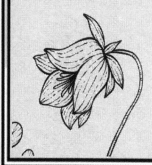

DAY 87
Guided by the Light

Psalm 119:105 (NIV)
"Your word is a lamp for my feet, a light on my path."

Devotional

Psalm 119:105 is a beloved verse that offers profound insight into the guiding power of God's Word. In a world often shrouded in darkness and confusion, this verse assures us that God's Word provides clarity and direction for our lives.

"Your word is a lamp for my feet" speaks to the practical and immediate guidance that Scripture offers. In ancient times, a lamp was essential for navigating the darkness, helping people avoid obstacles and find their way. Similarly, God's Word illuminates our daily paths, providing guidance for each step we take. It helps us to make choices that align with His will and to avoid the pitfalls of life.

"A light on my path" expands on this imagery, suggesting that Scripture not only guides us in immediate decisions but also provides overarching direction for our journey. Just as a light reveals the broader landscape, God's Word offers wisdom for understanding our purpose and direction in life. It helps us to see beyond the immediate and to align our lives with His greater plan.

This verse invites us to reflect on the role of Scripture in our own lives. Are we allowing God's Word to light our path and guide our decisions? Are we using it as a source of wisdom and direction, or are we relying solely on our own understanding?

Prayer

Heavenly Father,
Thank You for Your Word, which is a lamp to my feet and a light to my path. Help me to seek Your guidance in all areas of my life and to trust in the clarity and direction that Your Word provides. May I follow Your path with confidence, knowing that You illuminate my journey. Guide me in Your truth and help me to share Your light with others.
In Jesus' name, Amen.

CONTEMPLATION

Spend a few moments in quiet reflection, visualizing how God's Word is lighting your path. Consider the areas where you need guidance and ask God to reveal His direction through His Word. Allow the assurance of His light to fill you with peace and confidence.

DAY 88
Healer and Savior

Matthew 8:16-17 (NIV)

"When evening came, many who were demon-possessed were brought to him; and he drove out the spirits with a word and healed all the sick. This was to fulfill what was spoken through the prophet Isaiah: 'He took up our infirmities and bore our diseases.'"

Devotional

Matthew 8:16-17 reveals a profound truth about Jesus Christ's ministry on earth. This passage not only highlights His power to heal and deliver but also underscores the fulfillment of ancient prophecies that speak of His redemptive work.

"When evening came, many who were demon-possessed were brought to him" illustrates the depth of human suffering and desperation. People came to Jesus with their physical and spiritual afflictions, seeking relief from their burdens. This scene is a powerful reminder that Jesus welcomes all who are in need, regardless of their condition or the severity of their suffering.

"He drove out the spirits with a word and healed all the sick" demonstrates Jesus' authority and compassion. His ability to heal and cast out demons with just a word shows that His power is both immediate and effective. It also reflects His deep compassion for the suffering and His desire to restore wholeness to those who are broken.

"This was to fulfill what was spoken through the prophet Isaiah" connects Jesus' actions to the prophetic promises of the Old Testament. The reference to Isaiah 53:4, "He took up our infirmities and bore our diseases," confirms that Jesus is the fulfillment of God's promises for healing and redemption. He did not just come to offer temporary relief but to bear the weight of our suffering and to bring ultimate healing.

Prayer

Dear Lord Jesus,

Thank You for Your power to heal and for taking up our infirmities and bearing our diseases. I bring before You the areas in my life where I need Your healing touch. Help me to trust in Your compassion and the promises fulfilled through Your sacrifice. May Your work in my life be a testimony to Your grace and love. Guide me to extend this hope to others who are in need of Your healing.

In Jesus' name, Amen.

CONTEMPLATION

Take a moment to sit quietly, focusing on the areas where you need healing. Visualize Jesus bearing your burdens and feel His compassion surrounding you. Allow the assurance of His fulfillment of the promises to fill you with peace and hope.

DAY 89
Courage in God's Faithfulness

Deuteronomy 31:6 (NIV)
"Be strong and courageous. Do not be afraid or terrified because of them, for the Lord your God goes with you; he will never leave you nor forsake you."

Devotional

Deuteronomy 31:6 is a powerful reminder of God's unwavering presence and His call for us to live boldly and courageously. As Moses prepared to hand over leadership to Joshua and as the Israelites faced the daunting task of entering the Promised Land, this verse encapsulated the assurance they needed.

"Be strong and courageous" is a command and encouragement combined. It calls us to face our challenges with bravery, not relying on our own strength alone but drawing upon the strength that God provides. Courage is not the absence of fear but the willingness to act in the face of it. This command reminds us that God expects us to act bravely because He equips us for the task.

"Do not be afraid or terrified because of them" acknowledges the reality of fear and intimidation. Whether facing difficult situations, daunting decisions, or adversaries, it's natural to feel afraid. However, God's command is to not let fear dominate our hearts or paralyze our actions.

"For the Lord your God goes with you; he will never leave you nor forsake you" offers the assurance that we are never alone. God's constant presence provides the ultimate source of strength and comfort. The promise of His presence means that we can step forward with confidence, knowing that He is with us every step of the way, guiding, protecting, and supporting us.

Prayer

Heavenly Father,
I thank You for the promise that You will never leave me nor forsake me. Help me to be strong and courageous in the face of my fears and challenges. May Your presence be a constant source of comfort and strength in my life. Teach me to trust in Your faithfulness and to act boldly in accordance with Your will. As I move forward, let Your peace and courage guide my steps.
In Jesus' name, Amen.

CONTEMPLATION

Take a few moments to meditate on areas where you need courage. Visualize God's presence accompanying you, and allow His promise to fill you with peace and resolve. Trust in His unwavering support as you face your challenges.

DAY 90
Seeking His Kingdom First

Luke 12:31 (NIV)
"But seek his kingdom, and these things will be given to you as well."

Devotional

Luke 12:31 offers a profound yet simple directive from Jesus: "But seek his kingdom, and these things will be given to you as well." This verse encapsulates a key aspect of living a life centered on God's priorities and His promises.

In the context of this verse, Jesus is addressing concerns about material needs and anxieties over daily provisions. He encourages us not to be preoccupied with the things of this world but to shift our focus towards the eternal and spiritual realm of God's kingdom. The promise here is that when we prioritize God's kingdom, our earthly needs will be met.

"But seek his kingdom" is an invitation to align our hearts and lives with God's will and purposes. Seeking God's kingdom means pursuing His righteousness, embracing His values, and actively participating in His work on earth. It involves putting God first in every area of our lives—our goals, decisions, and relationships.

"And these things will be given to you as well" reassures us that God is attentive to our needs. When we make His kingdom our priority, He promises to take care of our other needs. This doesn't necessarily mean that every desire will be fulfilled exactly as we envision, but it does mean that God will provide for what we genuinely need in accordance with His perfect plan and timing.

Prayer

Heavenly Father,
I thank You for the promise that when I seek Your kingdom first, You will take care of my needs. Help me to shift my focus from earthly worries to Your eternal purposes. Teach me to trust in Your provision and to prioritize Your will in my life. May my actions and decisions reflect a heart that seeks Your kingdom above all else.
In Jesus' name, Amen.

CONTEMPLATION

Spend a few moments in quiet reflection, asking God to reveal areas where you may need to refocus on His kingdom. Consider practical steps you can take to prioritize Him in your daily life and trust in His provision.

DAY 91
Faithfulness in God's Promises

2 Timothy 2:13 (ESV)
"If we are faithless, he remains faithful, for he cannot deny himself."

Devotional

2 Timothy 2:13 offers a profound truth about God's unwavering faithfulness. This verse reassures us that even when we falter in our faith, God remains steadfast and true.

"If we are faithless" acknowledges the reality that our faith can waver. Life's challenges, doubts, and trials can sometimes shake our confidence. We may struggle to hold onto our faith amidst uncertainty, fear, or discouragement. However, this verse provides a powerful counterpoint to our human frailty.

"He remains faithful" is a comforting assurance that God's faithfulness is not dependent on our own. His character and promises are constant and unchanging. God's faithfulness is a reflection of His nature—He is always true to His word and His commitments. No matter how we may falter, His love and promises endure.

"For he cannot deny himself" underscores the essence of God's nature. Faithfulness is an intrinsic part of who God is. He cannot act contrary to His character. This truth means that His promises, His love, and His commitment to us remain intact regardless of our circumstances or our shortcomings.

Prayer

Dear Heavenly Father,
I thank You for Your steadfast faithfulness. Even when my faith wavers, I am comforted by the truth that You remain true to Your promises and to Your nature. Help me to trust in Your unchanging love and to hold fast to Your word. Strengthen my faith and let Your faithfulness be a source of hope and encouragement in my life. May I also share this assurance with others who need to hear of Your unwavering commitment.
In Jesus' name, Amen.

CONTEMPLATION

Take a few moments to reflect on areas where your faith may be struggling. Meditate on God's promise of faithfulness and allow His unchanging nature to strengthen and renew your trust in Him.

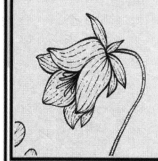

DAY 92
The Giver of Every Good Gift

James 1:17 (NIV)
"Every good and perfect gift is from above, coming down from the Father of the heavenly lights, who does not change like shifting shadows."

Devotional

James 1:17 is a profound reminder of the nature of our Heavenly Father. It assures us that every blessing and every gift we receive is a direct result of God's generosity. The verse highlights three crucial aspects of God's gifts:

EVERY GOOD AND PERFECT GIFT: The verse starts by emphasizing that all good and perfect gifts come from God. This includes not only tangible blessings but also the intangible ones—love, grace, peace, and wisdom. When we experience joy, growth, or comfort, it is an indication of God's hand in our lives.

FROM ABOVE: God is the source of all that is good. This truth can be comforting, especially when we face challenges or uncertainties. It reminds us that our Father, who is in Heaven, is always involved in our lives, providing for our needs and blessing us with gifts that nurture our spiritual and emotional well-being.

UNCHANGING NATURE: The verse concludes by describing God as the "Father of the heavenly lights, who does not change like shifting shadows." Unlike the world around us, which is often unpredictable and ever-changing, God's character remains constant. His love, generosity, and faithfulness are unwavering. This stability provides us with a solid foundation in times of doubt or difficulty.

Prayer

Heavenly Father,
Thank You for being the source of every good and perfect gift in
my life. I am grateful for Your unwavering love and constant
presence. Help me to recognize and appreciate Your blessings
daily, and grant me the strength to trust in Your unchanging
nature. Teach me to share Your generosity with others,
reflecting Your grace in my actions.
In Jesus' name, Amen.

CONTEMPLATION

Take a few moments to meditate on the verse, allowing
its truth to sink deep into your heart. Reflect on how
you've seen God's gifts in your life today and how you
can trust in His unchanging nature throughout your
day.

DAY 93
The Faithfulness of God

Psalm 40:5 (NIV)
"Many, Lord my God, are the wonders you have done, the things you planned for us no one can recount to you; were I to speak and tell of your deeds, they would be too many to declare."

Devotional

Psalm 40:5 is a beautiful declaration of God's immeasurable goodness and faithfulness. David's words in this verse remind us of the countless ways God has acted in our lives and in the world. This verse is a powerful testament to the abundance of God's works and His unwavering commitment to His people.

"Many, Lord my God, are the wonders you have done" reflects a heart that is overwhelmed by the sheer magnitude of God's actions. David recognizes that God's deeds are not only numerous but also extraordinary. Each wonder and miracle, from creation to personal experiences of grace and deliverance, is a testament to God's power and love.

"The things you planned for us no one can recount to you" speaks to the depth and complexity of God's plans. His intentions for us are beyond our full comprehension. Even if we tried to articulate every blessing, provision, and guiding hand, it would still fall short of capturing the fullness of His work in our lives.

"Were I to speak and tell of your deeds, they would be too many to declare" illustrates the overwhelming nature of God's goodness. His actions in our lives are so abundant that they cannot be fully expressed. This realization calls us to live with a heart of gratitude, acknowledging that God's blessings are both countless and immeasurable.

Prayer

Dear Lord,
I am in awe of the many wonders You have done and the plans
You have for me. Your deeds are beyond measure, and I am
grateful for every blessing and guidance You provide. Help me
to cultivate a heart of gratitude and to trust in Your good plans
for my life. May I share Your goodness with others and
recognize Your abundant love and faithfulness in all
circumstances.
In Jesus' name, Amen.

CONTEMPLATION

Spend a few moments in silent reflection,
acknowledging the countless ways God has worked in
your life. Allow yourself to be overwhelmed by His
goodness and let this awareness fill you with gratitude
and joy.

DAY 94
The Power of Faith

Matthew 17:19-20 (NIV)

"Then the disciples came to Jesus in private and asked, 'Why couldn't we drive it out?' He replied, 'Because you have so little faith. Truly I tell you, if you have faith as small as a mustard seed, you can say to this mountain, "Move from here to there," and it will move. Nothing will be impossible for you.'"

Devotional

In this passage, the disciples are perplexed. They had tried to cast out a demon but failed. They came to Jesus privately, seeking understanding and guidance. Jesus' response offers profound insight into the nature of faith and its power.

FAITH AS SMALL AS A MUSTARD SEED: Jesus uses the mustard seed as a metaphor for faith. Though small in size, a mustard seed holds the potential for significant growth. This illustrates that even a small amount of genuine faith can have a tremendous impact. It is not the quantity of faith that matters but its authenticity and sincerity.

THE POWER OF FAITH: Jesus emphasizes that even a small amount of true faith is powerful enough to accomplish what seems impossible. Just as a mustard seed can grow into a large tree, a small measure of faith in God can lead to remarkable outcomes. Faith in God enables us to face challenges, overcome obstacles, and experience the miraculous.

OVERCOMING DOUBTS: The disciples' failure to cast out the demon was not due to a lack of effort but a lack of faith. Jesus' teaching underscores the importance of relying on God's power rather than our own abilities. When we confront seemingly insurmountable challenges, it's crucial to place our trust in God's strength and not be swayed by doubts or fears.

Prayer

Lord Jesus,
I thank You for the powerful reminder that even a small amount of faith can achieve the impossible. Help me to nurture and grow my faith, trusting in Your strength and power rather than my own. When faced with challenges, grant me the courage to act in faith and to rely on Your promises. Strengthen my belief and use it to overcome obstacles and bless others.
In Your name, Amen.

CONTEMPLATION

Take a moment to silently meditate on how Jesus' words apply to your life today. Reflect on areas where you need to trust God more fully and how you can allow even a small measure of faith to bring about change.

DAY 95
God's Invitation to Seek and Find

Jeremiah 33:3 (NIV)
"Call to me and I will answer you and tell you great and unsearchable things you do not know."

Devotional

Jeremiah 33:3 is a powerful promise from God that invites us into a deeper relationship with Him. In this verse, God extends a personal invitation to each of us: to call upon Him and to seek His wisdom and guidance. The verse offers us three profound assurances:

CALL TO ME: God's invitation to "call to me" is an open and inclusive one. No matter where we are in life or how we feel, we are invited to reach out to Him. This call is not limited by our circumstances or our state of mind. It's a reminder that God is always accessible, ready to listen and respond.

I WILL ANSWER YOU: God promises to answer our calls. This assurance is comforting, especially when we feel uncertain or alone. His responses may not always come in the form we expect, but He is always present, ready to guide us. His answers come with divine wisdom and understanding, tailored to our needs.

GREAT AND UNSEARCHABLE THINGS: God promises to reveal "great and unsearchable things" that are beyond our current understanding. This highlights the limitless nature of God's knowledge and His desire to share profound insights with us. As we seek Him, He will reveal truths and guidance that exceed our own wisdom and understanding.

Prayer

Heavenly Father,
I thank You for Your invitation to call upon You and Your promise to answer. I am grateful for Your willingness to reveal great and unsearchable things to me. Help me to seek You earnestly, trust in Your timing, and remain open to the wisdom You provide. Guide me in my journey and grant me the understanding I need to navigate life's challenges.
In Jesus' name, Amen.

CONTEMPLATION

Spend a few moments in quiet reflection, asking God to reveal His wisdom to you. Consider any areas in your life where you need guidance and invite Him to speak into those situations. Trust in His promise to answer and guide you.

DAY 96
Beyond Our Imagination

Ephesians 3:20 (NIV)
"Now to him who is able to do immeasurably more than all we ask or imagine, according to his power that is at work within us."

Devotional

Ephesians 3:20 is a vibrant reminder of the limitless nature of God's power and His ability to exceed our expectations. This verse is a profound declaration of God's capabilities and an invitation to trust in His abundant provision. It offers us three significant assurances:

IMMEASURABLY MORE: The verse starts with an assurance of God's ability to do "immeasurably more" than we can ask or imagine. This emphasizes that God's power is beyond our ability to fully comprehend or measure. No matter how grand our dreams or how specific our requests, God's answers and blessings can surpass them.

ACCORDING TO HIS POWER: The verse underscores that this extraordinary capability is "according to His power" that is at work within us. It's not about our own strength or resources but about God's divine power operating in our lives. This power is the same that raised Jesus from the dead and is active in transforming and empowering us.

AT WORK WITHIN US: God's power is not distant or detached but actively working within us. This means that as believers, we have access to His incredible power daily. It's a power that can bring about change, overcome obstacles, and fulfill purposes beyond what we could ever achieve on our own.

Prayer

Heavenly Father,
I am amazed by Your promise to do immeasurably more than I
can ask or imagine. Thank You for the power that is at work
within me through Your Holy Spirit. Help me to trust in Your
limitless capabilities and to seek Your guidance in every aspect
of my life. Expand my vision and faith, and let me see Your
power at work in ways that exceed my expectations.
In Jesus' name, Amen.

CONTEMPLATION

Spend a few moments in silent prayer, asking God to
reveal areas in your life where you might be limiting
His power. Open your heart to His possibilities and
trust that He can achieve far more than you could ever
envision.

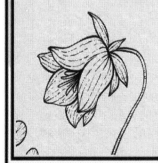

DAY 97
Beauty for Ashes

Isaiah 61:3 (NLT)

"To all who mourn in Israel, he will give a crown of beauty for ashes, a joyous blessing instead of mourning, festive praise instead of despair. In their righteousness, they will be like great oaks that the Lord has planted for his own glory."

Devotional

Isaiah 61:3 is a profound promise of transformation and renewal. It speaks to the heart of God's redemptive work in our lives, offering a powerful exchange for our pain and suffering. This verse provides three key assurances:

A CROWN OF BEAUTY FOR ASHES: God promises to replace our ashes—symbols of mourning and loss—with a crown of beauty. In ancient times, ashes were associated with grief and repentance. This divine exchange signifies that God can take our deepest hurts and transform them into something beautiful. His promise is not just about alleviating suffering but about creating something new and magnificent from our brokenness.

A JOYOUS BLESSING INSTEAD OF MOURNING: The verse assures that God will replace mourning with a joyous blessing. This doesn't mean that our pain will be erased instantly, but that God will infuse our lives with joy and hope despite our sorrows. His blessings are designed to uplift us, offering comfort and encouragement even in the midst of challenges.

FESTIVE PRAISE INSTEAD OF DESPAIR: God promises to replace despair with festive praise. Despair can weigh heavily on our spirits, but God provides a new song for us to sing—a song of celebration and gratitude. This transformation leads us to a place where we can genuinely worship and praise Him, acknowledging His goodness and faithfulness.

Prayer

Heavenly Father,
Thank You for the promise of exchanging my ashes for beauty
and my mourning for joy. I bring before You the areas of my life
where I feel broken and in despair. I trust in Your power to
transform these places and to fill them with Your blessings.
Help me to embrace the joy You provide and to offer You praise,
even in the midst of trials.
In Jesus' name, Amen.

CONTEMPLATION

Spend a few moments in quiet reflection, asking God to
reveal areas where He wants to bring transformation
in your life. Allow yourself to feel His comfort and
embrace the new beauty He is creating from your
ashes.

DAY 98
The Strong Tower

Proverbs 18:10 (NIV)
"The name of the Lord is a strong tower; the righteous run to it and are safe."

Devotional

Proverbs 18:10 offers a vivid image of God as our refuge and strength. This verse illustrates the safety and security found in God's name, emphasizing His role as a protector in times of trouble. It provides three key insights into the comfort and safety we have in Him:

THE NAME OF THE LORD: The "name of the Lord" in Scripture represents His character, authority, and presence. It is not merely a title but a declaration of His divine nature and promises. Invoking God's name is a recognition of His power and His ability to intervene in our lives. It is a name that embodies His faithfulness, love, and sovereignty.

A STRONG TOWER: God is likened to a "strong tower," which is a symbol of security and protection. In ancient times, a tower was a fortified structure that provided safety and refuge from enemies. Similarly, God is our fortress, offering a place of safety from the storms and adversities of life. His strength and stability are unwavering, giving us a secure place to find refuge.

THE RIGHTEOUS RUN TO IT AND ARE SAFE: The verse reassures us that those who seek refuge in God—those who are righteous, or aligned with His will—find safety and protection. Running to God in times of trouble is an act of faith, demonstrating our trust in His ability to guard and deliver us. When we turn to Him, we are shielded from the dangers and uncertainties that life may bring.

Prayer

Heavenly Father,
I thank You for being my strong tower and refuge. I am grateful
for the safety and security I find in Your name. Help me to run
to You in times of trouble, knowing that I am protected by Your
strength. Guide me to live confidently under Your care and to
share Your refuge with others who are in need.
In Jesus' name, Amen.

CONTEMPLATION

Take a moment to reflect quietly on the areas of your
life where you need God's protection. Ask Him to be
your strong tower in these areas and to remind you of
His steadfast presence and security.

DAY 99
Unfailing Faithfulness

1 Samuel 12:22 (NIV)
"For the sake of His great name the Lord will not reject His people, because the Lord was pleased to make you his own."

Devotional

1 Samuel 12:22 is a powerful reminder of God's unwavering commitment and faithfulness to His people. This verse comes at a moment when the Israelites were concerned about their standing with God, especially after their request for a king and their subsequent actions. The verse provides three crucial insights into God's nature and our relationship with Him:

FOR THE SAKE OF HIS GREAT NAME: God's commitment to His people is anchored in His great name. This reflects His character, reputation, and the promises He has made. God's name is synonymous with His faithfulness, honor, and integrity. Because of who He is, He will not forsake us. His actions are driven by His desire to uphold His name and His promises.

THE LORD WILL NOT REJECT HIS PEOPLE: Despite our shortcomings and failures, God remains steadfast in His love and commitment. The verse reassures us that no matter how we may falter, God's rejection is not part of His plan. He remains devoted to us, always ready to extend grace and restoration. His loyalty is not conditional upon our perfection but is a reflection of His eternal nature.

PLEASED TO MAKE YOU HIS OWN: God finds joy and satisfaction in making us His own. This speaks to the depth of His love and the value He places on each one of us. Being God's own is a privilege and a sign of His deep affection. It underscores that our relationship with Him is not merely transactional but relational, filled with genuine care and delight.

Prayer

Heavenly Father,
I am grateful for Your unwavering faithfulness and Your promise to never reject me. Thank You for the joy You find in making me Your own. Help me to embrace Your love and trust in Your name. Strengthen my faith and enable me to extend the same grace to others.
In Jesus' name, Amen.

CONTEMPLATION

Spend a few moments in quiet reflection, acknowledging God's steadfast love and commitment to you. Ask Him to help you fully grasp and live out the assurance that He will never reject you, and to find comfort in being His own.

DAY 100
Abundant Blessings

Deuteronomy 28:2 (NIV)
"All these blessings will come upon you and accompany you if you obey the Lord your God."

Devotional

Deuteronomy 28:2 highlights a profound promise of God's blessings upon those who obey Him. This verse is nestled within a chapter that outlines the blessings for obedience and the curses for disobedience, emphasizing the profound impact of our choices on our experience of God's favor. It provides three key insights into how we can experience God's abundant blessings:

GOD'S PROMISE OF BLESSINGS: The verse begins with a powerful affirmation that blessings will come upon us. These blessings are not random or arbitrary but are a direct result of living in alignment with God's will. God's blessings encompass not just material prosperity but also spiritual and relational well-being. They are a reflection of His favor and love for His people.

THE ROLE OF OBEDIENCE: The promise of blessings is conditional upon obedience to the Lord. Obedience is more than mere compliance; it is a heartfelt response to God's love and commandments. It involves living in accordance with His teachings and seeking to align our lives with His desires. When we obey, we open ourselves to receive the fullness of His blessings.

ACCOMPANIED BY BLESSINGS: The verse assures us that blessings will not only come upon us but will also accompany us. This means that God's favor will be a constant presence in our lives, guiding and enriching us in every aspect. It signifies that God's blessings are not temporary or fleeting but will remain with us as we continue to follow Him.

Prayer

Heavenly Father,

Thank You for Your promise that blessings will come upon me and accompany me when I obey You. Help me to live in accordance with Your will and to embrace the blessings You have for me. Guide me to be a reflection of Your favor in my interactions with others and to share Your love and grace.
In Jesus' name, Amen.

CONTEMPLATION

Spend a few moments in quiet reflection, considering how God's blessings have been evident in your life. Ask Him to help you live in a way that continues to invite His favor and to guide you in recognizing the blessings that accompany your obedience.

NOTES

NOTES

NOTES

NOTES

NOTES

NOTES

NOTES

NOTES

NOTES

NOTES

NOTES

NOTES

NOTES

NOTES

NOTES

NOTES

NOTES

NOTES

NOTES

NOTES

Made in the USA
Columbia, SC
02 January 2025

50956462R10126